My Journey Home

100 Years of Walking with the Lord

~An Autobiography~

Mamie Parker Williams

as told to Louis F. Morgan

Published by Derek Press
Cleveland, Tennessee

Cover design by R. Ariel Vázquez

Unless otherwise noted, Scripture quotations are from the King James Version of the Holy Bible.

ISBN: 0-87148-092-1

To order additional copies of this book, write to:
Morgantown Church of God
32 Magnolia Street
Morgantown, Mississippi 39483

This book is lovingly dedicated
in memory of

General Grant Williams

1901 — 1989

who, being empowered by the Holy Spirit,
served his fellow man with compassion,
integrity, character, and dedication
as a minister to broken spirits,
counselor, pastor, and
true friend.

From the General Overseer

September 13, 2001

Mrs. Mamie Parker Williams
Morgantown Church of God
32 Magnolia Street
Morgantown, MS 39483

Dear Sister Williams:

Happy birthday and congratulations on this 100th year of your notable and worthy service to God, family, and the Church of God.

On behalf of the Executive Committee, the International Church of God family located here in Cleveland, Tennessee, and the extended church family—which has come into existence for the most part since you were first baptized with the Holy Ghost and began playing the organ and teaching in our Sunday schools—I express a debt of gratitude for all the years, the prayers, and the service you have rendered.

In terms of the New Testament it appears that only John the Beloved was graced of God to live a century and it was he who expressed most beautifully the Lord's promises for what lies ahead. He recorded our Lord's most reassuring words—*"In my Father's house are many mansions: if it were not so, I would have told you. I go to prepare a place for you. And if I go and prepare a place for you, I will come again, and receive you unto myself; that where I am, there ye may be also"* (John 14:2, 3)—and gave us a vision of what is to come—*"And I saw a new heaven and a new earth ... the holy city, new Jerusalem, coming down from God out of heaven ... And God shall wipe away all tears ... and there shall be no more death, neither sorrow, nor crying, neither shall there be any more pain: for the former things are passed away"* (Revelation 21:1-5).

Today, as your brothers and sisters, we share your hope, your joy, and your prospects of an even brighter future.

Sincerely,
R. Lamar Vest
General Overseer

Author's Preface

Mamie Williams is a remarkable woman. I have known few individuals who possessed such a love for life or passion for serving Christ. Surely she draws from the reservoir of His strength and power. She is resilient, always bouncing back from hindrances tossed in her pathway. She is wise, imparting tried and true knowledge from her own experiences to anyone who will take the time to listen and learn. She is caring, wanting to encourage others to succeed in life and to live for the Lord.

As a child I lived a few houses away from Grant and Mamie Williams, whom I always referred to as "Brother" and "Sister" Williams. I vividly remember riding my bicycle to their home, running into the house using the back entrance, and sitting at their feet as they told me stories of the past. I never remember leaving their presence but what we had a time of prayer. I must admit that I often ran out of things to pray for long before them. At those moments I sat quietly and listened to them. I remember Sister Williams praying so earnestly while on her knees. Brother Williams, seated in his recliner, would shake and tremble under God's power. Raising his hands, he would speak in an unknown language as tears streamed down his face. There was a feeling in the room during those moments of prayer that humbled me. I knew we were in the presence of the Lord.

When I was 12 years old my immediate family stopped going to church. I continued to go but can remember feeling alone. We often concluded each worship service by praying around the altar at the front of the sanctuary. Kneeling down to pray, it would not take long until I felt hands on my back as others knelt to pray with me. Usually Sister Williams was on one side of me and "Aunt Ethel" Rials was on the other side. "Uncle Mack" Stringfield often prayed with me as well. In those moments I knew that someone cared about my spiritual life. Listening to the words that they prayed over me, I became confident that God was going to use me in His Kingdom work. Today I often remind Sister Williams of how her prayers encouraged me. And just as she motivated me to live righteously, she has done the same with countless others throughout her lifetime and ministry in so many places. I realize that her influence is a priceless blessing, and my life is richer because of it.

When Sister Williams turned 100 years old in 2001, I could think of no better gift to present to her than writing down her life story—her testimony of God's faithfulness. I spent several hours interviewing her, as well as researching Church of God documents, including the *Church of God Evangel*, to verify the accuracy of the information. I was awed by her impeccable memory, even down to minute details. Her children also shared stories with me that have been incorporated into this book. It is written in first-person, staying true to her tone and vernacular. Some parts of the book are verbatim from the transcripts of the audio and video recordings made while interviewing Sister Williams. It is presented to you with her blessing and with the hope that you will be encouraged and inspired by her story.

I wish to thank several individuals who have contributed to the publication of this book. Maxine Edwards, a daughter of Mamie Williams, spent several hours proofreading the initial manuscript for accuracy. Her attention to detail is greatly appreciated. My parents, Larry and Mary Ann Morgan, and my great aunt, Opal Morgan, have encouraged this endeavor. They, too, love and appreciate Sister Williams. Bill George, Wilma Amison, Wanda Griffith at Pathway Press have each encouraged this project. I appreciate their advice and friendship. Marcus and Janie Hand, my Sunday school teacher and special friends, always provide encouraging words about my writing projects. Dr. David G. Roebuck, director of the Dixon Pentecostal Research Center, for his devotion in maintaining the Church of God archives. That collection was very helpful in verifying the information contained in this book. Steve and Emily Bullins (and Reed, Chandler, and baby Evan), whose friendship is such an important part of my life. Finally, special thanks to Jerry Puckett, R. Ariel Vázquez, and Oreeda Burnette for overseeing the publication of this book and its layout and design.

As you will soon learn from the following pages, Mamie Williams is a special person. She is a gift from God to us—a light that has shined upon our pathway. Yet, she is also an ordinary woman. She would tell you that she is like you and me. What makes her life so meaningful and inspiring is what the Lord has accomplished through her, and that has only been possible because she chose to surrender herself to His will for her life. She found her purpose in Him, which included being a loving mother, devoted wife and helpmate to her husband, and a positive Christian witness and minister in her own right. Each step of her journey has added to this remarkable story. And, until her earthly journey has ended, I'm sure she will continue to encourage and inspire many others while on her journey home.

It is her prayer, and mine, that you will be inspired and blessed by her testimony.

Louis F. Morgan
Cleveland, Tennessee
June 27, 2004

Introduction

My Journey Home ~ 100 Years of Walking with the Lord is the inspiring life story of Mamie Parker Williams. Born in 1901, Mamie enjoyed a childhood typical of rural Mississippi life. One of twelve children, she performed her role on the family's farm by picking cotton, working in a garden, and tending to a wide variety of farm animals. Her vivid memories reveal much about farm and rural community life at the turn of the Twentieth Century.

In addition, Mamie grew up in a Christian home and was converted in the Baptist church at age 16. Later, she became curious after learning that two women neighbors had spoken in an unknown language while in prayer. Then when the *Church of God Evangel* circulated through the community, the neighbors understood what they had experienced, and Mamie became the first young person in her community to be baptized in the Holy Spirit. She immediately began teaching a young people's Sunday school class and working to establish a local Church of God. She also felt called to assist in revival meetings by playing the organ and praying with seekers in the altar. She had begun her spiritual journey.

Upon leaving for her first revival, Mamie was given the choice between her family or her faith. Heartbroken, she knew that she must chose to walk in the path on which God was leading her. She left home and spent the summer working in revivals. Upon returning to the family homeplace, she was happily received by those who had initially turned her away. She began family devotions in her home, and ultimately led her relatives into the Pentecostal experience.

In 1923 Mamie met Grant Williams, a minister and graduate of the Church of God Bible Training School (now Lee University). They married a few months later and had a large family of eight children. Sister Williams' descendants now total more than 125.

Grant and Mamie planted and pastored notable congregations in Louisiana, Michigan, South Carolina, Tennessee, West Virginia, and primarily Mississippi. Also, in the early 1930s Reverend Williams was appointed as state overseer for Mississippi. When he passed away in 1989, he was the second-oldest credentialed minister in the Church of God at the time. Mamie's reflections reveal valuable insight about the Church of God from its early days of evangelism until the present. There are stories of remarkable conversion experiences, divine healing, and important lessons learned over the years.

Although Sister Williams is the oldest resident of Morgantown, she still faithfully attends services at the Morgantown Church of God. Growing older has slowed her pace, but it has not hindered her from ministering. She is still passionate about evangelism and seeing individuals enter into a personal relationship with Jesus Christ through the power of the Holy Spirit. For more than 85 years she has actively ministered the Word of God as the Lord has directed her path. She has viewed firsthand the power of God's Spirit thrusting the Church of God into an international movement with numerous ministries. Even at her advanced age, she is yielding to the Holy Spirit and faithfully goes forward, ever looking upward, on her journey home.

This book chronicles the life of Mamie Parker Williams in her own words. Assisted by Louis F. Morgan, Mamie Williams shares interesting stories of many noted Church of God people, as well as her own experiences as a mother raising eight children and assisting her husband in church work. True to her style, it includes helpful advice and personal testimonies scattered throughout its pages. *My Journey Home* is sure to entertain, enlighten and inspire you in your own spiritual journey with God.

Table of Contents

1

A Journey Begins

Life is often likened to a journey, at least that is the way I have always viewed it. Our earthly journey is simply preparation for our grand entrance into our eternal home. If that is the case, then I must really be slow at preparing—for I have been on my journey home for one whole century! However, I like to think that the Lord has me here to do a work for Him, thus explaining my longevity. Nonetheless, living to be one hundred years old is difficult to comprehend, at least to me. "Have I really been here this long?" I sometimes ask myself. I wonder where all the time has gone because many of the events of my lifetime seem to have happened only a few days ago. There is no doubt that I am very blessed. Just taking a moment to reminisce confirms that. My life has been an interesting journey filled with many people who have helped guide me and brought me much joy and happiness. While it seems like a short trip to me, I suppose that I really have been on a long journey home.

"Where is home?" you ask. Well, I can tell you that it is not the town in which I was born nor the town where I now live nor any place in between. Home to me is where Jesus Christ is, and according to the Bible it is a place called Heaven. This is the very reason that I have enjoyed living for the past 100 years. I have understood that there is much more to life than just what we see or experience around us (although I have enjoyed most of that too). Yet, I am hoping, looking and expecting the Lord to soon say, "Come up a little higher." I anticipate the day when "the Lord himself shall descend from heaven with a shout, with the voice of the archangel, and with the trump of God: and the dead in Christ shall rise first: Then we which are alive and remain shall be caught up together with them in the clouds, to meet the Lord in the air: and so shall we ever be with the Lord" (1 Thessalonians 4:16, 17). When that day comes this journey as I now know it will have ended and an even more exciting one will have begun. I will finally be reunited with all my friends and loved ones who have already crossed over before me. And, most importantly, I will finally see Jesus and share in the glory of my eternal home. But until He calls me away, I am going to continue doing all I can for Him while traveling toward Heaven.

My journey began on September 13, 1901, near Vardaman (Calhoun County), Mississippi. I was the seventh child born to Robert and Mattie Lee Parker and given the name Mamie Jane Parker. In all, there were 12 children in this family, each born near the town of Vardaman in northern Mississippi. All of the children in order are Archie, Willie, Clara Hayes, Burrel, Vador Stewart, Clarence, me, Roy, Rena Winters, Tommy Lee, Lillian Vanlandingham and Tilmon. So as you can see, I did not begin my journey alone. I had a large, loving family with me. And that is the way it has been all my life.

2

Papa was a Planter

My papa, Robert Parker, owned a 160-acre farm near Vardaman, Mississippi. When I was born they called him a planter, but most people know that occupation simply as a farmer. We children helped on the farm to raise every kind of animal that one could imagine having on a farm back in those days. We had ducks, geese, turkeys, sheep, chickens, cows, horses, hogs and goats. I remember how the chickens would wake us up every morning with their cackling in the hen house. We also had large cotton crops and a regular garden. I always loved how pretty the cotton was just before we picked it. It looked as if the fields were covered with a fresh snow. The fresh vegetables in the garden were also bountiful. I remember how the corn seemed to grow so tall, especially when I was just a small child. Everything seemed larger than life back then, but our family farm was always full of life.

We stayed busy with chores all year long too. If I was not working outside, I was inside helping my mama, Mattie Lee Parker. We were always cooking and cleaning. And we canned fresh fruits and vegetables in half-gallon jars. I can remember helping Mama with canning when I was very young. Sometimes I grew tired of canning, but it seemed worth it when we were able to enjoy seasonal food throughout the year. Mama always put up enough food to carry us through the winter. We had homemade brooms made out of straw that we tied together and used to sweep out the house and porch. We also had to scrub the floors with soap on special occasions and for our big cleaning time in the spring of each year. We hoed away weeds from the garden and sometimes even in the cotton fields, as well as from the yard surrounding the house if the goats did not manage to eat it all. I helped gather eggs from the hen house, and we had to be careful not to pick up snakes that sometimes gathered in the chicken nests as well. I took my turn milking the cows and feeding all of the animals. My brothers and Papa did much of the most strenuous labor, such as plowing the fields, planting the crops, repairing buildings and baling hay. But as we girls grew older we also carried our weight of the hard work. The whole family worked on the farm, and that is how we spent much of our time. Our mornings came early, but we enjoyed being with each other. I learned at an early age the importance of a family and the benefits of working together.

I especially remember how busy the farm was every year when the cotton crop was ready. It was usually near the end of summer and around the first day of fall that we worked so hard picking cotton. All the family helped in some way, and the younger children usually brought us water. We had cotton bags and baskets that we carried with us as we went down the rows. Once we had filled our bag, we emptied it into a big wagon. When we were finished Papa took the cotton to a gin at Vardaman. After Papa sold the cotton, he would go pay his taxes and buy a barrel of flour, a fifty-pound bag of sugar, and other things like that from the stores in Vardaman or Calhoun City.

Our house was the largest building on the farm and consisted of three bedrooms, a parlor and a family room. We had a large front porch, a large breezeway ran though the center of the house, and a small porch connected the main house to the kitchen in the back. We also had a large barn, the hen house, a smokehouse, and an outhouse. We never had indoor plumbing in my home when I was a child.

I remember the farm as being a wonderful place, even though the chores were not easy to complete. I especially loved being outside. I spent many days roaming through the open fields and woodlands that belonged to Papa. We even had streams and natural springs at various places on the farm. On summer days it was enjoyable to run through the cool waters of the stream, and spring was always beautiful with wild flowers blooming everywhere. I loved my old home place, and I loved Mama and Papa.

Papa was a good man. He was not able to obtain much formal education, but he was wise in many ways. He was also very skilled with his hands. I was especially impressed with the fences he constructed. The more I remember all the things he built I am amazed at how he did it.

My brother Roy, who was the next child after me, died from diphtheria when he was nine months old. Papa built the coffin himself and a neighbor decorated the inside of the coffin. In those days people usually decorated the inside of coffins for adults with black, but for Baby Roy they chose blue. Papa and other members of the family placed Roy in the coffin, loaded it on the wagon, and then drove the wagon to the church house for the funeral. It was a different time back in those days, and farm life required us to do many things on our own. Yet, it actually taught me many things that helped me all through my life.

Papa was a man of few words, but we knew that he meant what he said. He was firm in his correction. If he said to do something, we knew to do it. It wasn't because he was mean to us but just because he believed that children should obey their parents, and he wanted us to be good children. He was not a very religious man as some consider religion. He was very personal in that area of his life. However, he encouraged us to go to church and he would attend the "protracted meetings" (or summer revivals) with us at nearby churches. Mama and we children attended the Baptist church regularly, but we often attended the Methodist revivals each year and Papa went with us. I remember that he would not miss one of those services. He finished his chores early and cleaned up so that he could take us to the meetings every evening. I remember feeling happy when Papa took us to church. I would look out of the buggy and smile as I watched the dust fly behind our buggy wheels as we hurried down the road. Sometimes I would just look up at Papa and smile.

My papa was not a very affectionate man. I cannot remember him kissing us children or hugging us during our childhood. Yet, we knew that he loved us. It was something that was evident in the way that he cared for us and in the small things that he did for us every day.

Where Papa was not as open with his affection, Mama made up for it. She was able to show her love and affection more openly. What I remember most about Mama was her humility. And yet, she took great pride in her family. She might not have boasted to others about us, but she let us know that she was proud of us. She was such a good person and a devoted wife and mother.

Mama had a sister named Mollie and they were both orphans who had been raised by distant relatives. Mama did not seem to know much about her family, other than they were from North Carolina. Most of what I know about her was after the time she met and married Papa. He was older than her and I believe she was about 15 when they married. Papa was born on May 8, 1856, and Mama was born on February 14, 1870. We never knew much of either of our extended families. Back then families did not get together like we are able to today unless they went by train or buggy. And there was not much time to be traveling because keeping up the farm and taking care of a family was more than a full-time job. And even though Mama tended to the house chores, she also worked outside on the farm. She was not afraid to work, and I think that helped us girls understand our responsibility to work on the farm as well.

I also remember how we kids would have to share a bed. There were two main bedrooms for us kids, one for the boys and one for the girls. Each had a fireplace and two beds. Although the boys and the girls slept in different rooms, we did not necessarily have the same people sleeping together every night. Basically, it was just who ever got to bed first. But I remember how happy our home was and how much we loved each other. We were typical children with disagreements, but we really did have a happy home.

I was blessed with wonderful parents. I think of them often and can see them so plainly in my mind. There is Papa, smiling at me from under his puffy white mustache, working in the field while wearing his pants and suspenders with a long-sleeved shirt. (He never wore overalls; always suspenders and pants. Once my brothers bought him a suit, but he never wore it. Mama suggested that he was saving it to be buried in, but Papa spoke up and said, "I ain't even gonna wear it then!") My sons Davis and Royce took after Papa in their looks. I can also see Mama in my memories, always wearing her long dresses with her hair pulled back and a bright smile on her face. She was part Indian (Native American) too.

I am thankful for my parents. Today many children do not have the blessing of having both a mother and father in the same household. That grieves my heart because I know how important it was for me to have the support of both my Papa and Mama. I am eager to see them again; I miss them so much. Just a few nights ago I even dreamed about them. It will not be long until I see them again when I finally make it home. And, I imagine that Papa will even greet me with a hug and kiss!

3

A Child at Play

Growing up near the town of Vardaman was fascinating to me. We lived out in the country in a community often referred to as Taylor. But Vardaman always had plenty of people, especially on Saturdays. That is when many of the people living in the country rode into town. There was a beautiful town square with shops outlining its four sides. Most of the businesses were located in that section of the center of town. I also remember the livery stable where horses where kept and sold, a train depot and a shop that sold pretty dresses and fancy hats and shoes. Of course, back then we did not travel too much. Sometimes we would travel a little farther to Calhoun City. It also had a town square set up with the intention of building the county courthouse in the middle of the square. However, the town of Pittsboro became the county seat and is where the courthouse was built. I always thought this was odd, because Calhoun City was actually larger than Pittsboro.

Calhoun City had more shops than Vardaman did, as well as another shop with pretty dresses, although I never bought any of them. There was no need for those fancy dresses on the farm. Sometimes we took the buggy to Calhoun City and spent the day. But those days did not come often. Most of our life revolved around the farm and our friends and family there.

When I was growing up our nearest neighbors was the Free family. My brothers and sisters and I spent many hours with the Free boys and girls. Maggie Free was nearest my age and we had much fun playing together. Sometimes her sisters Lorene and Vianna joined us too, but usually it was just Maggie and me. We swam together in the creeks and ran through the fields picking flowers or wild blackberries. We rode horses and even milked cows together. We were best friends.

I also had fun with my brothers and sisters. Some of my brothers and sisters had already married and left home to have families of their own, but there was still a house full of activity at the old home place. Once my sister Vador came back to the home place to visit. She was older than me and had already married. This was during World War One and her husband was overseas in the military service. Vador was missing him greatly on this particular day, so she decided to visit with us. When it came time for her to leave, I wanted to take her home in the buggy. I was just a young girl, but Vador was willing to let me drive her home. Back then we had two female horses, mares we called them, which we hooked up to the buggy. I harnessed up one of the horses myself but did not tie up the usual harness string. (This is was a strong string that pulled the buggy.) Instead, I just used a regular string. While going up the hill the string broke and the buggy started rolling back downhill. The old mare got scared and she started kicking and raring. For a moment we were scared, but we quickly jumped out and stopped the buggy. Finally we found some strong string and hooked the buggy back up to the old mare. Vador eventually made it home. There was always something happening around the farm to create excitement and provide us with much laughter.

All my siblings attended the same school that I did. It was located in a little village called Lloyd. We often walked to and from the old school building with the Free children. It was about a two-mile walk, rain or shine. Some of our subjects were reading, spelling, recitation (speech), history, and arithmetic. They also taught us about writing and we learned many patriotic things about the Untied States. Back then we started each morning with prayer and by reciting the Pledge of Allegiance in unison while facing the American flag. (However, I remember that we did not use the same words that are in the pledge today, but I cannot remember exactly what we said. Too, there were not as many stars on the flag to represent the number of states. I can remember flags having both 46 and 48 stars when I was a student.) Often our teacher even shared Christian devotions as well. Our school building was only one large room with several windows and a potbellied stove. The teacher had a desk at the front of the room and had a large board she wrote on with chalk. (One of our punishments was washing chalk away from the blackboard, but I never remember getting into trouble in school.) We shared desks with someone else, and I always tried to sit with Maggie Free.

Finally they got a school nearer to our home and classes were offered through the eighth grade. This was known as Taylor Schoolhouse. The Free children also went to this school, and I was glad. I was blessed to be able to complete the eighth grade. This was really an honor considering that many children were often forced to quit school and help more on the farm. My parents believed that it was important for us to learn, especially Papa. I suppose that he wanted us to have more of an education than he had received.

The highlights of my childhood were the times spent together in the family room of our house. While we were not exactly wealthy, we did have a nice house. Usually we gathered together in the family room in the evenings. If we were entertaining company, we often sat in this room as well. Of course our parents were almost always with us. Sometimes Mama would knit and Papa would play the fiddle. We would read and spend time talking with each other in this room. We had kerosene lamps for lighting and a fireplace for the winter days and cool spring evenings.

I remember how Papa would take out the violin in the evenings and begin to play while Mama and we children sat and listened. Sometimes my brother Burrell would join Papa and play the organ. Burrell could also play the Autoharp. It was during these times that I learned about music. I also learned how to play the piano and organ. I still love to play these instruments even after a century of living.

Sometimes, if the song was really upbeat, we children would like to jump around and dance. I remember once when I was courting a beau, or boyfriend as it is termed now. There were several of us young people sitting in the family room. Papa had taken out the violin and my brother Burrell was playing the organ. I decided that I wanted to dance. My beau, Oran Spratlin, told me not to dance, but I could not sit still any longer. I jumped up and proceeded to dance. My boyfriend was so upset about it that he broke up with me! I guess he thought I was just showing out, and I might have been.

I enjoyed my childhood. There was much work to do and the labor was sometimes difficult, but we were a family. We were together. We looked out for each other and our life revolved around one another—family and friends. Throughout my life I have been blessed with this same kind of friendship in the many friends that I have made along my journey.

4

Awakened by the Spirit

I grew up in a Christian home. My parents were of the Baptist tradition. Although Mama attended church regularly, Papa typically attended only during protracted meetings and special services. But I was taught to have a personal relationship with Jesus Christ, to honor His Word as recorded in the Bible, and to love my neighbors. I was also taught that the church sanctuary was a sacred place for reflection, fellowship and worship.

When I was 16 years old I realized that I was a sinner. This was during a revival at the Baptist church and I felt the conviction of the Holy Spirit. I asked the Lord Jesus to forgive me of my sin and save my soul. His Word teaches us that if we repent He will forgive us. I then accepted His grace and love and committed my life to Him. This was in the Loyd Missionary Baptist Church, located near the school our family attended. I joined this church during that revival. There was also a Methodist church in this community.

I was happy in my Christian experience and also lived a good life before my family and friends. I tried to be faithful in my childish way. Later I was happy that I had earned a good witness before others, especially when I experienced a deeper measure of God that was quite unfamiliar to most of the people in our community.

The first time I heard about the baptism of the Holy Ghost was in 1919, although at the time I did not understand exactly what it was all about. It was during a revival at the Loyd Missionary Baptist

Church. Katie Free was the first to receive the infilling of the Holy Spirit, but she (nor anyone else) did not understand what she had experienced. She received the Spirit-baptism while praying at home with her sister-in-law (who was also my sister-in-law), Vera Parker. While praying, Katie began to speak fluently in a language that she had never heard before. The words just began to flow through her. It was quite odd, but Katie knew that she had received something from the Lord. Soon afterward Vera Parker also received the Holy Ghost. They began telling everyone what had happened to them and would get together to pray, rejoice and speak in tongues. But neither really understood what they had experienced except that they were certain it was from the Lord.

Then, an old Brother Alexander received a copy of the *Church of God Evangel* from some of his relatives. After he finished reading it he brought it to the Baptist revival service and gave it to Katie following the meeting one evening. I was there that night. She read the headline out loud, "People are receiving the Holy Ghost and speaking in other tongues." Then she read aloud the scripture that was printed under the headline: "'And they were all filled with the Holy Ghost, and began to speak with other tongues, as the Spirit gave them utterance.' - Acts 2:4." She began shouting and cried out, "Oh, I know now what I have! I know now what I have!" That was all the light that she had on being baptized with the Holy Ghost, but she shouted and praised God that night in the church house. Then she began speaking in tongues and even gave an interpretation to what the Holy Spirit had spoken through her in the other language. That caused people to believe that she really had something from God, including me. We had sanctified people in our community, but Katie was the first holiness [or Pentecostal] person that I ever knew about.

I got a chance to look at that issue of the *Church of God Evangel* and read all of the testimonies of other people who had this same experience. I began to hunger in my soul to also receive this "baptism of the Holy Ghost." We wanted to know more, but there were no Pentecostal churches nearby. Our only source for learning more about the truth was the Bible and the *Church of God Evangel*. How we loved to get copies of the *Evangel*! I remember that we were all so hungry for more of God and to learn more about His power. We wanted to be closer to Christ. We had just a taste of His presence and we longed for more.

Request for Prayer

Dear Evangel *Readers Everywhere:*

I am not a member of the Church of God, neither does the Holy Ghost abide.

I joined the Baptist church a number of years ago and have since been trying to live a life that would please God. But, friends, I haven't done enough yet. Since I began reading the Evangel *I have seen more of the light of God. I want the saints one and all to pray earnestly for me that the Holy Ghost may abide and speak in other tongues. As the Spirit gives the utterance.*

My heart's desire is to be a true and shining light for my Savior and lead lost souls to Him. I realize that the coming of Christ will not be long and Oh! How my heart aches for those that are lost. I want the power of God so that I can tell the lost world more about our precious Savior.

Oh! Friends, pray for me that I may have this blessed experience that leads our souls to know more about Christ.

I am seeking full salvation and hope to soon let the Evangel *readers know that I have it.*

Love to all,
Mamie Parker

Church of God Evangel—*June 5, 1920*

Eventually we got in touch with Brother E. C. Rider, a Church of God preacher. He came to our community during the summer of 1920 and conducted a two-week meeting at the Taylor School House. The Baptist church would not let us hold service in the church house because the pastor was skeptical of speaking in tongues. Later our little band of believers faced much persecution and criticism from both the Baptist and Methodist churches nearby. We did not want to cause trouble for the established churches, nor were we against them. We just knew from reading the *Evangel* and from the two experiences within our own community that God was blessing in a powerful way in accordance with the Bible. We had to know more about the Pentecostal blessing.

Brother Rider was the first Pentecostal preacher that I ever met. He never did pastor the local church at Taylor, but he would come periodically and hold revival meetings—especially during the summer. He was conducting the meeting on the day that I received the baptism of the Holy Ghost, which was during his first revival in our community in the summer of 1920.

I will never forget that service. After Pentecost first came into our community and I saw the light on the baptism of Holy Ghost, I became hungry for the blessing. The first time I went to the altar, Sister Katie Free and Sister Vera Parker knelt beside me and prayed with me. We prayed for several minutes, and I wept before the Lord as I praised the name of Jesus and sought to be filled with the Holy Ghost. I wanted all of the relationship with God that the Bible says a Christian should have, and I so wanted to receive the Holy Ghost. Brother Rider laid his hands on my forehead and began to pray for me as well. I heard them speaking in tongues and their bodies would shiver and tremble under the power of the Holy Ghost as they prayed for me. I could feel the presence of the Lord so strongly. After a while of praying I felt a powerful anointing of God, and I experienced what seemed to be a cleansing inside my soul. I felt so clean inside. They told me that I had been sanctified and the Lord was preparing me for the Holy Ghost to abide within. I left that first meeting without receiving the Holy Ghost. That night as I went to bed I prayed for God to fill me with His Spirit. I knew it was His will for me to have the Holy Ghost, and I fell asleep thanking Him for the wonderful feeling I had felt inside since praying in the altar that night.

The next day I attended service again. I hungered more for the Holy Ghost on this day than I ever had before. The second time that I went to the altar I remained there until I prayed through to the Holy Ghost and began to speak in other tongues as the Spirit enabled me. It felt like electricity flowing through my body. I cried tears of joy as the Holy Spirit spoke through me in a language that I had never heard before. At first it was just strange sounding syllables, but as I yielded my tongue and voice to the power of God the words began to flow. When I stood from the altar I knew that I had received the baptism of the Holy Ghost. I was so excited and I immediately had a yearning within my soul to tell others of this great experience and of my precious Jesus! I was the first young person in my community to receive the Spirit baptism, but I did not understand it all then. All I knew was that I felt like I could have floated on air, and I was completely in love with Jesus.

About a week after my birthday that year, Brother Rider returned to our community and conducted another ten days' meeting, after which he set the Church of God in order with ten members. Five of us had the Holy Ghost and Brother Rider baptized six of us in water. Then we shared in the Lord's Supper and feet washing before Brother Rider left our community. Oh, we had a time! We shouted and danced and praised the Lord. For so long we had depended solely upon the *Evangel* to gain added light into the way of Pentecost, but finally we had a church of our own in which to worship. We were so happy.

After the church was set in order many people received the blessing. Being the first young person in my community to receive the Holy Ghost, many other young people followed because of the life they saw that I was living. It was not because I was so good, but it was the God that was in me Who was so good. Many of them accepted the Lord through my testimony and work for the Lord. Pentecost was so new in our community until people did not understand it and did not know what it was all about, but soon the church began to grow and people came to know Christ in a very real and powerful way.

Different preachers visited us at first for several days' meeting. Sometimes it was a male evangelist and sometimes a female evangelist. Crowds gathered when they heard we were going to have services. Usually most all sermons dealt with what it meant to be "Holiness," which is what we called ourselves for believing in salvation, sanctification, the baptism of the Holy Ghost, divine healing, and the Church of God. Back then we were taught that the Church of God was the restoration of the Bible Church like the early apostles had experienced. Members generally believed that all Christians would ultimately come to understand the Pentecostal blessing and unite together in the Church of God. But even then I did not believe that Church of God people were the only Christians, I just felt that others had not seen the light on the baptism of the Holy Ghost and all God has for His children. But, most people did not understand what we believed and these sermons helped them see the light on Holiness. There was also much hard preaching against sin. Too often we unnecessarily preached against simple things, such as forbidding women to cut their hair or wear make-up. Women could only wear dresses and men could not even wear short-sleeved shirts in public. Neither could wear jewelry, not even a wedding band. We were taught that these were sinful and worldly, as well as such amusements as movie theaters, fairs, novel reading and even ballgames. These teachings were clearly unnecessary, but they did provide a shelter for us, especially our young people. We were so eager to live righteously that sometimes we added unnecessary excesses in our Christian practice. Nonetheless, we were preaching the truth of God's Word and spreading the message of the full gospel. Despite our simplicity, God still blessed us and used us mightily.

I can remember how large numbers of people would stand outside of the school building and look through the windows to watch us worship. We would dance and shout as we worshiped the Lord. Often people stood to testify of how God had blessed them in some way such as healing their body, saving them from sin, filling them with the Holy Ghost, or just meeting a multitude of other personal needs. People would become so overwhelmed with the presence of the Holy Spirit that sometimes they would fall out in the altar and even in the pews where they were sitting. We called this being "slain in the Spirit," although they were not actually killed. Many times when they came to themselves they told of visions, being healed, or receiving the Holy Ghost.

Sometimes people came just to hear us sing. Oh, how we loved to sing! We would sing for long periods of time, and if people were being blessed we would sing the same song several times. Generally our music was upbeat and people enjoyed clapping their hands with the beat. Sometimes people would begin to dance and shout as we were singing, while others ran to the altar to be saved. The little school building would vibrate many times as our voices joined together in song and worship of the Lord.

Once when I was playing the organ during an altar service, the Holy Spirit was moving powerfully throughout the church. I was so overcome by the Holy Ghost that I lifted my hands toward heaven and rejoiced. I did not know what was happening all around me at that point because my mind was so focused on the Lord. However, they told me later that the organ kept playing on its own for the several minutes that I was rejoicing and not touching the keys. It is something that I cannot explain, but I have heard my brother testify to that spiritual wonder many times.

When people heard the sermons, and sometimes just during the singing, they often became convicted of their sinful ways. I remember them being so overwhelmed that they would literally run to the altar, screaming in agony. We would gather around them and pray with them until they were assured that they were saved or had received what they were seeking from the Lord. One thing that set us apart from other churches was the liberty in our services. While we had a usual order, everything was dependant upon the Holy Spirit. We also prayed aloud in unison often throughout the service. It was certainly different from church services to which I had always been accustomed, but it was indeed wonderful!

Often the schoolhouse was filled with people, and some were there to seek more of God and some were skeptics. Some came just so they could watch us and then criticize us throughout the community. But we were so full of the love of God that we paid them little attention. We knew that we had received something genuine from God and were determined to move forward with Him. Sometimes those who criticized us the most later found themselves to be some of our most dedicated members. Hardened sinners melted in the presence of the Lord. Some of the most unpleasant people I knew became as gentle and humble as lambs after receiving the baptism of the Holy Ghost.

Following the service in which I received the Holy Ghost, that night as I lit the kerosene lamp in the family room I told the family that I was going to have prayer. No one went to bed, but we all prayed together. Even Papa sat over in the corner by the fireplace until we were finished praying. I was the one who led the family in prayer that night and it continued for as long as I lived at home.

Socially, it was not easy for me when I first received the Holy Ghost. This seemed like a strange experience to most of my family and friends. But we all began to search the Scriptures and it revealed that the early apostles practiced this type of religion. The Book of Acts in the Bible was filled with people speaking in tongues as the Holy Spirit enabled them to do so. I also subscribed to the *Church of God Evangel* and discovered that people all over the world were being baptized with the Holy Ghost. And no one could convince me that what I felt in my soul was not genuine. I knew that there was a greater power at work in me than I had ever before experienced. I was burning with a passion to do more for God and tell others about Jesus. I still faced some trials, but Jesus seemed so real to me that the trials did not matter.

My friend Maggie Free had many questions for me. She wanted to know what it felt like and how I could speak in a language that I did not even know or understand. Each of us who had spoken in tongues had lived good, Christian lives previously, so that helped convince others that surely this blessing was genuine. Maggie knew that it was from God as well, and she began to ask the Lord to fill her with the Holy Ghost. I well remember the day Maggie received the Holy Ghost. It was during an altar service and she was sitting in my lap under a brush arbor. I believe this was during the revival that Brother G. C. Dunn conducted.

Following Maggie's Spirit-baptism, she began assisting me in working with young people. She began a class for children and encouraged them to raise money for missions and the orphans just as I had been doing with the older kids. She even began preaching some. I remember one time there was going to be a district meeting and our pastor asked each of us to preach. We were assigned topics, but I refused to preach because I did not think I was a capable speaker. Maggie went on and did her part. Many times I have suffered over that, because I feel that I did not do all that I could have done. I know now that I should have put aside my fear and done what was asked of me. It caused me much inner grief for quite some time after that.

Maggie later became a lady preacher and even married a Church of God minister, Brother P. W. Chesser. (Her brother-in-law, Brother H. L. Chesser, was once the general overseer of the Church of God.) Too, most of the Free family moved to Cleveland, Tennessee, and had positions with the Church of God. I remember that Vianna Free married Dwight Daniel. She worked at the general headquarters for the Church of God, and he worked at the church's publishing house. Their daughters (Patsy, Carnell, and Delilah) comprised a trio known as the Daniel Sisters. They sang with Otis McCoy, were on the radio, and became quite well known in Gospel music. But during those early days of ministry in our community, it was good to have a friend who shared the same experience with me. After Maggie received the blessing our friendship grew even stronger.

But not all friendships were enduring. My beau at the time was Arthur Spratlin, the older brother of the boy who had broken up with me when I had danced in my home quite some time earlier. Arthur was not sure how to react to the news that I had received some strange baptism. I remember the day that he came to call at the old home place. We sat in the family room and it was quite awkward. I tried to act as normal as I could, but he could clearly tell there was a difference in me. He was nice and tried to understand, but I knew that he was terribly confused. So, we eventually broke up as a result. I heard that Arthur later told someone, "Well, she looks like Mamie, but she sure don't act like Mamie." I will have to admit that much had changed in my life. I became consumed with the desire to minister for the Lord. I wanted to tell everyone about Jesus and His love and power. My whole wants and plans for life had suddenly been abandoned. All I wanted was to be closer to Jesus and spread His Word.

Mama was also confused. She just did not know what to think or say. But after she watched me for a while she knew that God was at work in my life. Sometime after my infilling, Mama went down into the woods in front of the house to pray. There she received the Holy Ghost baptism and also spoke in unknown tongues. But Papa never did. At least, if he did he never let me know. Papa was always quiet about his faith. But I suspect if he had ever received the Holy Ghost he would not have been able to keep it quiet. I have often seen the Holy Spirit transform shy people into very outgoing preachers after they received their Spirit-baptism.

Back in those days we did not realize that the Pentecostal blessing had been poured out in Mississippi for many years, nor had we heard of the wonderful Azusa Street Revival that occurred in Los Angeles, California, in 1906. Later we learned that Pentecostalism had entered Mississippi as a result of the Azusa Street Revival. We also heard that the Church of God was first introduced in Mississippi in the spring of 1909 when Reverend L. P. Adams from Memphis, Tennessee, preached at the Stonefield tabernacle near Cascilla, just south of Charleston. That is when Sister Clara Priest was baptized with the Holy Ghost and her experience stirred the community for miles. Later the first Church of God in Mississippi was organized in August of 1912 near Enid, Mississippi, just north of Charleston. It is still active today and is known as Friendship Church of God. In 1915 Reverend Warren E. Evans first introduced the Church of God into southern Mississippi at Morgantown. He was a drunkard who had moved to Florida, but after getting there he began attending the Church of God and was saved, sanctified, baptized with the Holy Ghost, and delivered from alcohol. He then returned to Mississippi to preach about the blessing to his family. For many years, the Charleston and Morgantown areas were where most of the Church of God activity was centered in Mississippi. However, other churches began springing up throughout the state just as ours did near Vardaman. And, much like us, they did not realize that so many others also shared our experience in Mississippi. It was just so new to us at the time. However, through the years we learned more about the history of others receiving the blessings all throughout the Church from the time of the apostles. But back when I first received the Holy Ghost we only knew of our experiences and of those similar through the testimonies and reports that we read in the *Church of God Evangel*.

5

Obeying the Call of God

When I received the baptism of the Holy Ghost, I began teaching in church and playing the organ for services. Back then we just had a pump-organ and occasionally someone would have a guitar. I was burdened to work with young people, especially my friends. Since I was the first young person in my community to receive the Holy Ghost, I was anxious for others to also receive the blessing. So, I began teaching the young people's Sunday school class. Until I got married I had a Sunday school class of between 20 and 30 young people at my home church, the Taylor Church of God near Vardaman. Some of the family names for my students were Free, Parker, Tallent, Taylor, Vanlandingham, and Willis.

I was always interested in missions and orphans. I taught my class with an emphasis on these two ministries as well. Often we would raise money to send to the church headquarters for missionaries and the orphanage. It was important to me that young people learned early to support these projects and to learn the importance of giving to the Lord's work. I have had this goal in mind since I first started teaching Sunday school over 80 years ago.

One year after I received the Holy Ghost I felt led to go into the ministerial work. Mama had received the Holy Ghost by this time and she understood, but not Papa. He could not understand how a woman could preach or be active in ministry. But I knew that God was calling me to assist in revivals and that I must obey. Finally the day came in the summer of 1921 when I was to leave home for a revival meeting. When I walked out on the doorstep, one of the neighbor boys was there to take me to the train station. Papa looked at me and said, "If you go, you need not come back." It was the point in my life where I truly had to commit to the work of the Lord.

It was tough to leave home, especially without Papa's blessing. But I knew that God was calling me into ministry. I could not afford to disobey the Lord. I took the train to Thorn, Mississippi, where I met three other women ministers: Nell Lovett, Mildred Biggers, and Sister Lou Lamb. Nell was what we considered back then to be an "old maid," but she was the leader among women ministers in the Church of God in Mississippi at that time. She was from Sapa, Mississippi. Mildred Biggers lived near Ackerman, Mississippi, in the same community with the noted Blackwood family. (The Blackwoods were active in the Church of God as preachers and singers. Members of this family eventually organized the internationally known "Blackwood Brothers Quartet.") All of these ladies were older than me, and at the time only Sister Lou Lamb was married. Her husband was a doctor in the town of Artesia, Mississippi, and Sister Lamb had several children. (However, after our ministry team broke up, Mildred and Nell both later married.)

Each of these women was actively involved in preaching, but I felt led to help in the meetings by playing the organ and praying with people in the altar services. We each had traveled to Thorn to assist Brother G. C. Dunn and his wife, Mirtie, in a revival. I was also able to teach some of the young people. As usual, I tried to encourage them to be missions-minded and to remember the orphanage. Those were always special topics to me. I still believe the Bible gives us special instructions concerning those ministries.

We had a wonderful revival at Thorn, which is located near Houston, Mississippi. I remember that a teenage girl named Mary Wimberley was healed during this revival, as well as others. But my heart was always tender toward young people and I especially remember her healing. The Lord touched her eyes and she did not have to wear glasses any longer. This meeting was very successful. About thirty were saved and filled with the Holy Ghost. Brother Dunn baptized about 25 in water and set the church in order with 39 members just before the summer revival season ended. We spent the entire summer there working in the revival and witnessing throughout the community. That congregation has always been a strong church in Mississippi.

I stayed away from Vardaman all summer, but when the revival was over I decided to return to the old home place. I was not certain if Papa was angry with me, but I knew that the family would receive me back—even Papa. I was nervous inside and my heart raced as I walked down the road with suitcase in hand. "What if Papa is angry with me?" I thought. "What if he will not even speak to me?" The feeling was almost unbearable as I walked that long journey home. But I prayed and asked the Lord to be with me and to help my family understand. I knew that I was doing what God wanted and I had to trust Him to work it out.

It was not long until I could see the familiar sights. There was the woodland on one side of the road and the old home place on the other. The old home place in the distance was a welcomed sight! There was the field where Papa spent many hours—and so did the rest of the family, but not as much as Papa did. As I looked farther into the field I saw him. There was Papa. When he caught a glimpse of me, he quickly ran to meet me in the front yard. Now you must remember that Papa had never been a very affectionate man. I was certain of his love while growing up, but affection was a rarity. However, on this day he kissed my face and tightly embraced me as he welcomed me home. From then on Papa never objected to me going and helping in revivals. The other children never seemed to resent it either. They had to do extra work all of the summer because I was gone, but they seemed to know that I had this calling and never complained. They were happy to see me return home, and so was Mama.

I continued to travel and worked more than two years helping in revivals with Nell, Mildred and Sister Lamb. We were a noted ministry team in northern Mississippi. Nell did most of the preaching. My job was to play the organ and lead the singing. Not many churches had pianos or other instruments like we do today. So I carried a pump organ to the meetings. It was just a little organ you could carry around like a suitcase. I also worked in the altar and have always enjoyed praying with people who were seeking more of God.

When we traveled to different communities we would have to stay in the homes of church members. Many times we four women had to divide up and stay in different homes. It was quite different back then, but it was good to fellowship together. There was much love among the church people and everyone seemed to feel that what was theirs was also ours. No one had much to offer, but we all seemed to have enough.

Mildred was a good minister too. The summer after I received the Holy Ghost, she and Brother E. M. Washam, a young preacher from Eupora, came to my community and held a revival. I remember that we had a wonderful meeting that summer. Mildred cried a lot when she preached and could win more people to the Lord through crying and preaching than most any other preacher we had back then. I have often wondered just how many souls were birthed into the Kingdom of God through Mildred's tears. She just had a way of touching people.

We assisted several prominent ministers in the Church of God during that time. We were usually present and at our place of service for most of the major camp meetings and district conventions in northern Mississippi. We worked in meetings with preachers such as General Overseer A. J. Tomlinson, M.S. Lemons, J. B. Ellis, M. S. and Bertha Haynes, J. T. and Clara Priest, George B. Sprinkle, W. A. Capshaw and his daughter Jessie, Hal A. Pressgrove, the Moxley boys (J. R. and Luther), Joe W. Mullen, W. E. Raney, Brother and Sister E. K. Simpson, Lester Lay, C. A. Churchill, B. O. Funderburk, Joe Lentz, Z. D. Simpson, Jeff Musselwhite, Robert and Rene Blackwood and Roy Blackwood (who organized the quartet that later became famous around the world). There were many others that we assisted in their meetings, and I usually played the pump organ and always prayed with seekers in the altar. I can vividly remember a camp meeting conducted by Brother M. S. Lemons at the Stonefield tabernacle in Cascilla, Mississippi. It almost seems like it was just last week. I played the pump organ during those services, and we had a glorious time in that old tabernacle.

I remember another meeting at Stonefield tabernacle, which was located on a small hill with a creek flowing around it. Before the services many people gathered on the hillsides to pray. The men gathered on one side of the hill and the women gathered on the other. (Back in those days men and women often sat on different sides of the church as well.) During the prayer time one evening, I could hear Brother Joe Little praying aloud on the other side of the hill. He was really getting into his prayer. During service that night we had the usual testimony time before the singing. Brother Little became so excited during his testimony that he almost took over the service. He started walking out into the aisle and up near the front platform. He walked back and forth doing more preaching than testifying. I remember that he became so carried away in his testimony that he said, "Some people are like the Bible says, 'Straining at a gnat to swallow an elephant.'" He did not miss a blink and never even realized that what he said was unscriptural, at least until the next person testified and corrected the error. After service that night we all had a good laugh about it. Later, Brother Joe Little went to the Bible Training School in Cleveland, Tennessee. He became a well-respected minister in the Church of God. He was one of the first youth directors in Georgia and spent many years working in the church's publishing house in Cleveland, Tennessee. He and his wife, Myrtle, came to see my husband and me after we retired. We always thought so much of Brother and Sister Little. He was a humble minister who was known for his integrity.

One preacher came to us from Pennsylvania. Brother D. R. Moreland was to conduct a revival at Duck Hill, Mississippi, and we were to assist him. He came on the train and lost his ticket. He had to get off and get another ticket, but he wasn't exactly sure of the name of the town the meeting was in. The people at the train depot offered many suggestions, but nothing sounded right to Brother Moreland. Finally when they suggested Duck Hill, Brother Moreland shouted with excitement, "I knew it was some kind of an animal!" The Moreland family traveled together and was very musical. His daughter, Lourenna Smith, was also a preacher. But, on this particular occasion Brother Moreland was ministering in Mississippi alone.

Another interesting thing that happened to Brother Moreland while in Mississippi was when he first ate red pepper. We all knew that red pepper was very hot, but Brother Moreland did not. He took a big bite of the red pepper and made an awful reaction. He turned red-faced and exclaimed that he did not think he needed to taste any of the bad place! We all laughed. And that revival was very successful with many people being saved, sanctified, and baptized with the Holy Ghost.

Brother P. F. Fritz was another early minister that we assisted in revivals. He was not from Mississippi originally, but he pastored several churches in the state, including Stonefield, North Shady Grove, Cleveland, Morgantown, Mount Sinai, and Pickwick. Brother Fritz was a small man in stature, and he walked with a built-up shoe on one foot. A widower, Brother Fritz raised his young son, Harold, as a single parent. We assisted him in revivals at Stonefield, North Shady Grove, and Cleveland.

Brother C. A. Churchill was a Church of God preacher from Eupora, Mississippi, and was a great help in revivals around there. He was also a noted musician and songwriter. He played the organ in many of his meetings as well as preaching. But I always felt special when he would let me play the organ and lead singing during his meetings. His ministry was well known throughout the Church of God and he was requested for meetings in many states other than Mississippi.

I also enjoyed assisting in meetings conducted by Brother E. C. Rider, especially since he was the preacher when I received the Holy Ghost. Brother Rider was also the reason that I became acquainted with Grant Williams. Brother Rider knew both of us and worked it around that we met at the Church of God state convention in Cascilla, Mississippi. It was held in 1923 at the Stonefield Schoolhouse.

When I was back home, I continued to work in the local church that met at the Taylor Schoolhouse. I played the organ, was able to speak some, and taught the young people's Sunday school class. Of course, I was training them to give to the work of the Lord, support missions and care for orphans.

A Progressive Sunday School

I would just like to tell a little about our Sunday school at Taylor church. It has a number one Sunday school with eighty-five enrolled. All love the Church and its cause. We remember the orphans every Sunday and have our penny march and pay our pennies.

Class No. 2, of which I am teacher, never fails to respond. In this class we have thirty boys and girls enrolled, ranging from fourteen to twenty years. This class is taught to help the orphans and Foreign Missions. One of the boys recited the piece, China's Need. Then the class marched and paid their bit which amounted to $4.00. This class loves the Chinese and asks a blessing on those who are telling them the simple story of Jesus.

Yours for His cause,
Mamie Parker
Vardaman, Mississippi

Church of God Evangel — *July 7, 1923, page 3*

REPORT

The Church of God at Taylor reports victory. Children's Day was called for the third Sunday in June. It was a day of rejoicing for both young and old. The children spoke their pieces well. All seemed to honor "Him whom my soul loveth." A collection was taken for the orphans which amounted to $8.00. Many seemed to realize that the Church of God must do more for the orphans. Our pastor, J. E. Wigginton, preaches the Bible rightly divided and he believes in His church doing something for the orphans. God bless the orphans. We love them every one and our aim is to stand by them.

Mamie Parker
Vardaman, Mississippi

Church of God Evangel — *July 7, 1923, page 2*

6

Grant's Early Ministry

General Grant Williams was born on August 23, 1901, and grew up in Eupora, Mississippi. While no one really acknowledged him as "General Grant," some people referred to him as "G. G." and most called him "Grant." (But after our marriage I always called him "Daddy" and he called me "Mother.") He had a rough time growing up and lived with his mother, Jennie Whitaker, until he went to the Church of God Bible Training School. After he entered the evangelistic work, he did not live with his mother anymore but stayed mostly with an elderly couple, Brother and Sister J. C. Causey, near Gloster.

Grant was a young preacher in Mississippi, but he was well trained for Pentecostal ministers of his time. He received the Holy Ghost on December 28, 1916, when he was 15 years old. He felt the calling of God into ministry and, in the fall of 1918, enrolled in the second term of the Church of God Bible Training School in Cleveland, Tennessee. (This is now known as Lee University and located in the same city.) Classes for that second term began in November 1918. Grant earned distinction, and Sister Nora Chambers, the teacher, often referred to him as one of her best students. She admired Grant all of her life and he had great respect for her as well.

It was during Bible Training School that Grant studied more about the Bible, prophecy, music, and how to conduct evangelistic work. The students spent many hours studying the Scriptures, in prayerful intercession, and listening to Sister Chambers expound the Word of God. Grant often reminisced about the times that he and the other students wept before the Lord and prayed for hours at a time without ceasing. It was more than just book knowledge that they received in their training, it was also about how to be sensitive to the Holy Spirit and listen to His voice.

Many notable ministers personally mentored the students during this time, including General Overseer A. J. Tomlinson and bishops J. B. Ellis, F. J. Lee, M. S. Lemons, T. L. McLain, Sam C. Perry, and others. The classes met in an upper room at the Church of God Publishing House. There were only a few students during those early years, and Grant's first class included six others beside himself. They were: A. D. Evans (who married Brother Tomlinson's daughter, Iris), Stacy Miller, Earl Hamilton, J. Oscar Hamilton (who was also from Grant's hometown in Mississippi), Mary Howell and Bennie Terrell. Bennie, a young female evangelist, died of influenza just before Christmas during Grant's first term at BTS. This was during the influenza epidemic of 1918 that had spread across the country.

Grant completed three terms and part of a fourth term. Some of his other peers during those years were Jessie Penny, Elizabeth Gonia (who was almost twenty years older than Grant), George Danehower, Clarence Tarpley, Paul H. Walker, and Elmer Walker. Grant became very close to each of his peers, especially Oscar Hamilton and Paul H. Walker. Grant and Paul were the same age (actually Paul was about a month older), and Grant had been the second youngest pupil when he first arrived in 1918. He was seventeen years old then. Grant never missed one single day of class until he returned to Mississippi for Christmas in 1919. That was during the middle of the fifth term of the Bible Training School and Grant never returned. Instead, he began evangelizing throughout Mississippi. However, while he was still a student at BTS, Grant received his ministerial credential as an Evangelist in the Church of God on March 29, 1919. His home church at Eupora, Mississippi, set him forth into the ministry, and Brother A. J. Tomlinson signed his license.

Brother Williams had a hard life to live before he went into the ministry, and he had some tough times afterward. Some of his hardship was because he was so young and had accepted the call to preach. Some people felt like he was just a child, and in many ways he was, but Grant had a very anointed ministry. He worked with

Brother Hal Pressgrove, a state overseer in Mississippi during that time. Grant also had a lot of help from the elder ministers. There always seemed to be someone willing to help him and guide him in his youthful days.

One of those was Reverend J. T. Priest. He and Grant ministered in the same area of southwestern Mississippi for much of Grant's ministry before he married. They often teamed preached, along with Sister Clara Priest, in areas near Bude, Meadville, and Brookhaven. Often they walked to the places where they were conducting meetings. Once when Grant and Brother Priest were going to preach out in the country from Bude, Brother Priest had to make some homemade soles for his shoes. He said he had worn them out walking for the Lord!

When Grant was establishing the church at Bude, Mississippi, in 1921, he faced severe opposition. Once he was preaching in the local mill village at Bude. He had been preaching divine healing and many people were being healed. Others were laying down their medicine and trusting the Lord with their bodies. This did not make the local doctors happy. The town mayor, who happened to be a doctor, had the owner of the mill tell Grant that he could not preach at the company houses any longer.

After that, the Lord laid it on a man's heart to let Grant preach in his home. This was on the outskirts of town near a theater. Initially the services where held inside the house. However, the attendance soon outgrew the house and had to be held outside. Grant was preaching on the front porch of this man's home with the congregation scattered throughout the yard. The preaching soon started breaking up the theater. The law came and arrested Grant, charging him with disturbing the peace because of his loud preaching. Grant had to appear before a local judge. A friend of Grant's was knowledgeable of the law and instructed him to plead guilty of disturbing *their* peace. That is what Grant did, and the judge ordered him to pay a small fine. Realizing that Grant did not have the money and would have to go to jail, the judge passed around a hat in the courtroom to collect the money for the fine. There was more than enough money to meet the fine, and God had blessed Grant yet again for his faithfulness in preaching the Word. Many times later Grant remarked how he wished they had put him in jail so he could have preached to the people behind bars.

Finally, the people who had accepted the truth decided to build a tabernacle for Grant to preach in. When they completed the tabernacle Grant set the church in order. That was in the fall of 1921, and Grant continued to serve as their pastor until after our marriage. There is still a very active congregation at Bude today, and they always seemed to think so much of Brother Williams in that area.

Also at Bude church, Grant preached one night and three men got offended. They decided to whip him. The next day they met him on the road as he was riding into the city. They told him what they were planning to do to him, and he replied, "Boys I haven't done anything to you, and there is no way that I can take you by myself. But I guess you must do what you feel you have to do." Grant began to pray under his breath for the Lord to help him while the men began discussing their options. Grant heard one of the men say, "Well, he hasn't done anything to me." Then another man said, "Well he hasn't done anything to me either." So, the men decided that they would leave Grant alone, and one of them asked him where he was going. When he told them into town, one of the men wanted to know if he could ride with him. Grant agreed, and the man climbed into the buggy with him and rode to Natchez! That man became one of Grant's good friends.

Ministers today need to be thankful that they do not have the persecution like they did back in the days when they threw rocks into services, threw tomatoes and eggs, and most anything they could tempt you with. We had to preach from porches, under brush arbors, and sometimes even under the shade of trees. Grant knew that the gospel needed to be spread and where ever he could get a chance to preach the gospel, he did.

One of the highlights of Grant's early ministry was helping to "preach out" the McCall Creek Church of God near Bude, Mississippi. This church was organized in April 1921 with about 15 members. Brother J. R. Smith from Morgantown held the first meetings there, and Brother Williams followed him and preached for several days. Brother Williams was even challenged to handle a serpent one day during a service. Then Brother Jim Smith returned and set the church in order. McCall Creek is still an active church today.

Another place where Grant had a successful ministry was at Liberty, Mississippi. He set the church in order there known as Jacobs Tabernacle in 1920. Shortly after the church was established, a wonderful healing occurred. Kemble Jacobs was a little boy about

12 years old, and he came down with a very high fever. He was delirious for a while and his parents called for Grant to come and pray for him. Immediately the Lord healed little Kemble and sparked a revival in the community. During this revival Kemble and his mother both received the baptism of the Holy Ghost. His father, J. R. Jacobs, earnestly sought the blessing but never spoke in other tongues. He finally refused to eat until he had received the Holy Ghost. Within a short time the Lord filled Brother Jacobs with the blessing. He spoke in other tongues and even became a preacher. The Jacobs family was always very special to us.

Sometime later Grant began holding services near Gloster, Mississippi. He stayed in the home of Brother and Sister J. C. Causey during this time. By the spring of 1922, Grant had assembled several people who were interested in holiness. Brother M. S. Haynes, his wife Bertha and their daughter, Geneva, soon came and conducted a meeting for Brother Williams. Many experienced genuine revival and repentance during this meeting, with people becoming so full of the Holy Ghost that they began paying their debts and making restitution among their enemies. Many people were saved, sanctified and baptized with the Holy Ghost. Demons were also cast out during this meeting. After the Haynes family left, Grant continued to serve as pastor of the church and soon set it in order with about forty members. It was known as Union Church at that time. However, shortly after being set in order the church built a large tabernacle beside the public highway. The church then changed its name to Causey's Chapel.

It was also at Causey's Chapel that another wonderful healing took place. An infant child was deathly ill and the mother was not saved. She had only heard holiness preached once or twice before, but afterward had never attended the meetings again. However, when her child was at the point of death, she decided to call on the Pentecostal people because they strongly believed in divine healing. So, she called for Grant. He went to her home, anointed the little child, and prayed the prayer of faith. The baby was healed and the mother began attending church at Causey's Chapel. She was later saved and filled with the Holy Ghost. God loves his children so much, even when we do not always follow Him as closely as we should.

Following the establishment of the church at Gloster, Grant returned to Liberty to conduct a meeting. And, he still served as pastor at Causey's Chapel. Much like the work at Bude, Brother Williams also faced persecution while establishing the Rock Hill Church of God, located seven miles in the country from Liberty, Mississippi. Brother and Sister Joe Rushing were the only holiness people who lived in this community and they had earned a good reputation among the people. Grant visited in many homes throughout the area and preached on holiness and the Church of God. The meeting lasted for about two weeks. Others who assisted him in this meeting were Brother and Sister M. S. Haynes, J. R. Jacobs and J. T. and Clara Priest. However, it was after the first meeting had closed that the greatest revival occurred in the community. People began accepting the Lord, being sanctified and filled with the Holy Ghost and being healed. The community was stirred for miles and Brother Williams soon set the church in order. This was during the winter of 1922-23 and it was the last church that he established before we met.

Even after our marriage it was difficult for us at Rock Hill. I remember that there were some rough boys who often disturbed the services. Brother Robert Blackwood came and conducted a revival for us. As he was walking out of the door one of those rough boys knocked him down. The preachers eventually had to get the law to come to the services, and those rough boys said they were going to whip Grant.

We were strong in spirit at first, but then fear was trying to take root in us. One particular day I remember that Grant had worked hard during the day. Even though we were tired we felt that we must pray about the threats. We prayed until we got the victory! We tarried in prayer all through that night until God gave us a message that he was going to take care of us. After that we had no more fear of those boys, and they never did us any harm. We heard later in life that all three of those boys met violent deaths.

Grant had a successful ministry when we first met. The Lord had blessed him with opportunities to receive ministerial training and he had a love for people. His road was not an easy one to travel, but he was determined and faithful. God rewarded his efforts. Grant always was a fine preacher.

7

And the Two Shall Become One

I first met Grant Williams in May of 1923 at the Church of God state convention held at the Stonefield School House in Cascilla, Mississippi. Bishop A. J. Tomlinson, the general overseer of the Church of God, was the speaker for this meeting. Brother E. C. Rider worked it out for us to meet, and Sister Nell Lovett was in on it too. Nell and I traveled by train to Grenada, Mississippi. There, Grant picked us up in his one-seated Ford car and drove us to Stonefield. After we got to the church Nell and I were seated and Grant came and asked if he could sit next to me. Of course I said that he could. Following the service, he drove Nell and me to the place where we were staying. When the meeting had concluded, Grant drove Sister Nell Lovett and me back to Grenada, where we caught the train and went to her hometown of Sapa, Mississippi. This was in Webster County and near Grant's hometown of Eupora. I stayed there until the next state convention, which was held a few days later in Morgantown, Mississippi. When the time came for the next convention, Grant met us and drove Sister Lovett and myself to the meeting in his car. Now that was a sight to behold: the three of us riding all that distance in his one-seated car!

I remember when I first saw Morgantown. We arrived in time for service at the church, which was a white, frame building. I was impressed by the love among the people and their love for God. It was also rare that most everyone in the town belonged to the Church of God. We saw many people that we knew, including Hal Pressgrove, Robert and Ruby Price, J. T. and Clara Priest, J. Leon Thornhill, and many others that I would soon come to know and love. Since Grant was pastoring the churches in southern Mississippi, he seemed to know almost everyone at the meeting. Among those included Brother Warren Evans and his wife Nancy, Brother Quinnie C. Dunaway, Brother Jim Smith and his wife Ida, Brother Gene Morgan, and Brother Walter McNabb. Bishop Tomlinson was also preaching this convention as he had the one at Stonefield, and Brother E. C. Rider, our state overseer, was there as well.

Sister Lovett and Grant both stayed with families in Morgantown. However, I stayed in the home of Brother and Sister J. C. Lentz. He had been my former pastor and was then living near the Mount Sinai Church of God, located about five miles away from Morgantown.

After the meeting ended, Grant drove Sister Lovett and me back to her home at Sapa. During our ride Grant and I had a chance to talk about our lives and ministries. I knew in my heart that I wanted to marry him. Sometime before we reached Sapa, Grant and I became engaged to be married—sooner or later. Although we were not exactly sure when, we knew that the Lord wanted us together. It was just a good match, and it worked. I have often thought about how quickly we were engaged and married. I would not advise anyone to marry as quickly as I did, but somehow we knew that God wanted us together. And I am glad that God chose for us to be together. We shared a wonderful life.

In Eupora I boarded the train for Vardaman. During the train ride all I could think about was my new engagement. I could hardly wait to tell Mama. I was not going to be an "old maid." I was already borderline for becoming one, at least according to the custom in those days. If a woman had not married by the time she was twenty-five, then she was considered an "old maid." (I was twenty-two.) But that is not what God had in store for me. One day soon I would marry Grant.

I stepped off the train with Grant still on my mind. Then I heard a voice calling my name. I looked up and saw Clifton Hollingsworth. "Poor Clifton," I thought. I had forgotten all about him! He was my hometown beau. In fact, he helped pay my way to the state convention. Well, it was quite an ordeal explaining to him that I had met Grant and was engaged. But, somehow Clifton understood. He said that he could tell a difference in the way I looked and acted. I did not want to hurt Clifton, but I had met Grant and felt like he was the one the Lord wanted me to be with in life.

Grant had respect for Mama and Papa. Although I was 22 years old, he believed he had to ask their permission. I well remember when He went up to Papa and told him that he would like to marry me. Papa never had much to say, so he told Grant, "She's a woman of her own. If she makes her bed hard she'll have to lay in it." Papa said that because he was not going to object. Everyone looked at Grant as a young boy. He was twenty-two years old and just a kid in the eyes of most people. Yet, they had great respect for him as a preacher. I think Papa realized that too.

Grant and I married on August 30, 1923, at Taylor Church of God, which was my home church near Vardaman, Mississippi. Brother E. C. Rider, our state overseer, was supposed to perform the wedding. However, it had rained so until the roads were impassable and Brother Rider could not make it to the church in his car. Instead, we had a local Justice of the Peace to perform the ceremony, but we did have a church wedding. I still have one of my wedding gifts. It was a wedding book given to me by the daughter of Reverend M. S. Lemons. I ran across that little book just the other day (over 80 years after our marriage) and realized that I never took the time to fill it out!

After we married, I said goodbye to Papa, Mama, my family and church friends. Then Grant drove us to Gloster, Mississippi. There we stayed in the home of Brother and Sister Causey, the older couple with whom he had been living. When we got in the house Grant went into the bedroom and turned a somersault over the bed. I was accustomed to a little more dignity in my family and thought, "Good mercy! What kind of a preacher have I married to pull a stunt like that?" I said something to him about it and the woman of the house told me, "Now you let him alone. He belongs here."

It was during this time that Grant began to call me "Mother" and I started calling him "Daddy." I am uncertain if we acquired this from listening to the older couple with whom we were living, but those names continued for the rest of our marriage.

We continued to live with the Causey's and I remember being eager to assist Daddy in the three churches he had planted and was pastoring. I was pleased to be "Mrs. Grant Williams." I was happy to be married, and I was excited about a sharing a future ministry beside the man I loved.

8

Travels for the Lord

When Daddy and I married he was pastoring three churches, all of which he had organized. They were located at Gloster, Rock Hill and Bude, Mississippi. Although Daddy was not from this area originally, he was very well respected among these people in southern Mississippi. They had learned to love him ever since he first ministered there when traveling with Brother J. T. Priest, who had been the first minister appointed as bishop in the Church of God in Mississippi. And because the people loved Daddy so much, they were very accepting of me as well.

Shortly after I moved to Gloster with Daddy, we went swimming together in an old pond. I did not have a bathing suit, so I wore a pair of Daddy's pants. We could not let anyone see us because during that time the Church of God was strictly opposed to a woman wearing pants. It was grounds for dismissal from church membership. Now that would have been something if I had been turned out of the church, especially considering I was the pastor's wife!

We had a really good meeting at Gloster soon after we married. Our church was called Causey's Chapel. For about 10 days in September of 1923 Daddy conducted the meeting and did the preaching. I prayed with people in the altar and played the organ. Several people were healed during this meeting. Back then people testified of trusting the Lord with their bodies. That meant they did not believe in using any medicine or seeing a doctor when they got sick. Many Pentecostals were very strict on this line back in the early days, but God was faithful to us and He honored His Word. I have seen God perform some wonderful healings.

During this time many Church of God ministers preached "signs following believers" based on the passages in Mark 16:17, 18, 20: "And these signs shall follow them that believe; In my name shall they cast out devils; they shall speak with new tongues; They shall take up serpents; and if they drink any deadly thing, it shall not hurt them; they shall lay hands on the sick, and they shall recover.... And they went forth, and preached everywhere, the Lord working with them, and confirming the word with signs following."

Daddy also preached from this scripture often. At that time when he preached the Word, people really put him to the test. Sometimes it was church members and sometimes it was nonbelievers. People brought in poisonous serpents to the services and challenged Daddy to handle them. That happened during our first revival together at Causey's Chapel when a diamond-head moccasin was brought into the church. Daddy was challenged to handle it, which he did. But God never let any harm come more than what was a blessing in disguise. That was the first time that I was ever around serpent handling.

It all began during a night service of that revival when some outsiders brought a tied bag into the service and placed it on the platform. They told Daddy that it was a serpent and challenged him to handle the snake if he really believed what he was preaching. He pointed to the bag and asked the men, "Is the snake in here?" They confirmed that it was and eventually Daddy untied the bag. He poured it out onto the floor, except instead of a snake emptying onto the floor it was a frog. Daddy then made a spectacle of the outsiders and remarked, "Now what do you think about anybody that would lie like that?" He suggested that even they were too scared to pick up a serpent.

But that was not the end of that ordeal. They again challenged Daddy to handle a serpent, and this time it was an actual snake. Daddy took it up and handled it to demonstrate the power of God. While he was handling the snake it bit him on the finger and left fang marks. I really did not know what to think about it because I had never been around serpent handling before. But I trusted Daddy and felt that he knew what he was doing. I knew that if he did not believe God would protect him that he would not have taken up the snake. Some people wanted him to go to the doctor. I heard them say that he would be dead by morning, which made me concerned. But it was no more than if a pin had gone through his fingers, and he did not suffer from that at all. It disturbed me, but the Lord did protect him.

Another time, while at a revival in Dunn, Louisiana, in 1927, Daddy was again bitten by a serpent. He conducted a three weeks' meeting there, and after the first week unbelievers brought in the serpent and challenged him to take it up. Daddy took up the serpent and handled it for quite a while. Then it bit him on the left hand, causing his arm and hand to swell. He was in a great deal of pain and missed one day of the revival. They also wanted him to go to the doctor there, but he would not go. The next evening he got sick on his stomach and vomited up the poison. He said that the way he felt after he vomited up that poison was like a flower that needed rain and had been refreshed after a good shower. The next day you could not tell that anything was wrong with him, and Daddy preached each night for two more weeks.

There was also the time that Daddy was preaching in a church and someone threw a serpent onto the platform through the window. Daddy reached down, picked it up and put it in his coat pocket. He went right on preaching. After the service was over, we walked home. I thought about the snake and asked Daddy what he had done with it. "What snake?" he asked, at which time he felt it in his coat pocket. I never did see Daddy pull off his coat more quickly! Sure enough, the snake was still in the coat pocket.

In 1927 Daddy was preaching at the Louisiana state camp meeting, which was being held at the church in Epps, Louisiana. Also attending the meeting was Brother A. V. Beaube, who was just a young preacher then but eventually became a well-known minister in the Church of God. Brother J. C. Coats and his father, whom we called "Old Brother Coats," were attending as well. Both of the latter men had handled serpents before, and the younger Brother Coats was the state overseer of Texas. Of course the word got out and somebody brought a poisonous serpent into service one night. After the song service, the men prayed and felt like they had the anointing. They got the snake out of a bucket and the three of them on the platform passed it from one to the other just like you would pass a baby back and forth. I watched that snake slither up Daddy's arm quite a few times before he placed it back in the bucket. But, thankfully, it did not bite anybody. To my knowledge that was the last time that Daddy ever handled a serpent. That was in October of 1927.

I know that Daddy had handled snakes and fire before we married, especially around Bude, Meadville and at revivals in and around Morgantown. I had read about it in the *Church of God Evangel*, but I was not accustomed to this style of worship at my home church. They might have participated in such after I left, but it was a new practice to me when I married Daddy. I am glad that I was never tested in such a way. Thankfully, we no longer have to do that in our churches today. A lot of people talk about serpent handling today, but they have a different idea about it than the way it really was experienced by most of our early preachers. And today Pentecostalism is so widely known and accepted that no one challenges us with snakes…or frogs.

While we were pastoring our first churches immediately after our marriage in 1923, there was great turmoil in the Church of God. It was reported that General Overseer A. J. Tomlinson had misappropriated some of the church's money. It was an awful time as far as church government was concerned, but we kept on preaching and praying with people. Daddy said that it would all work out okay because God was in control of the Church. So we just prayed for God to work out the situation. But it did not get better until it got worse. Some churches supported Brother Tomlinson and some churches supported "The Elders." (That is what they were calling those who agreed with the Council of Twelve and felt that Brother Tomlinson had made some mistakes. Brother F. J. Lee stepped into the leadership for "the Elders.") Most of us were confused about all of the facts and what to believe. Brother Tomlinson had always been good to us. Daddy and I knew he loved the Church of God and, more importantly, the Lord. We could not believe that he would ever steal anything from the Church, although that is what some were saying in the local churches. Daddy said that was not true and that it was just a power struggle.

It might have all worked out okay, but then people began to be very divided over who was in charge of the church. Some preachers were going around preaching bad things about Brother Tomlinson and some were going around preaching bad things about "The Elders." It was a very painful time for all of our people back then. Daddy and I spent many nights crying and praying for healing in the church. But we never did stop loving people and preaching. Some people in both groups became bitter and preached that one group was the true church and not the other group, but we never did feel that way. We believed that we were all part of the Body of Christ. We decided to let the others argue if they wanted to, but we were going to pray and preach like we always had.

We went on to Cleveland, Tennessee, that year for the Assembly of 1923. At this point the churches had already divided, but the split was not totally complete. Daddy had decided to stay with the churches under Brother Tomlinson, who had been a great influence on him. When Daddy was a student at the Bible Training School there in Cleveland, he often visited in the Tomlinson home. You might say that he practically lived there when he was not in class or away preaching, although he slept in the boys sleeping quarters at the publishing house. The Tomlinson family always had people in their home and the Bible students spent much time with the Tomlinson children too.

While in Cleveland for the Assembly we were staying in the home of Brother A. J. Tomlinson. He was away at a meeting during that time, but his daughter, Iris, was there. Our plans were to attend the Assembly for the churches with Brother F. J. Lee (or "the Elders") and then stay on and attend the Assembly for the churches under Brother Tomlinson. At this time Daddy had decided to remain with Brother Tomlinson, but we still wanted to fellowship with our friends in "the Elders."

At some point during the meeting I became ill and stayed home one evening from the service. They were coming to a decision about splitting the church completely and somehow or other during that service Daddy became convinced that he should be with the churches under Brother F. J. Lee. He came home from the Assembly that night and told me, "Mother, I've decided to change over to the Elders." I told him that if he felt that was what God wanted then I was in agreement and would follow him. The next morning when we got up, we decided to leave early and head back to Mississippi. Daddy said there was no need to stay for the Assembly with Brother Tomlinson since he had decided to go with "the Elders." Plus, I was not feeling very well either. We went downstairs and Daddy told Iris that we had decided to change over. She was very sweet to us and replied, "Well, I pray you see your mistake. We hope you'll be satisfied."

When we returned to Mississippi we went back to the old home place to visit with my family. We stayed there a while and then went and visited a few days with Brother and Sister Causey. We never did go back to the churches that we were pastoring, but decided to let them choose for themselves whether to stay with Brother Tomlinson or join with Brother Lee. This left us without a church to pastor, but Daddy said that he was not going to be responsible for creating more division. Brother Tommy and Sister Clara Priest, who chose to remain with Brother Tomlinson, began pastoring the churches after we did not return. Gloster and Rock Hill eventually remained with Brother Tomlinson, but Bude chose to be under Brother F. J. Lee.

We returned to the old home place at Vardaman, and soon afterward I became pregnant. We were still without a church, but we knew some people in the Delta who made big cotton crops. They really loved Daddy and welcomed us to stay on their farm. Daddy accepted. I stayed at the old home place with Mama and Papa while Brother Williams went to make a cotton crop in the Delta. When it came time for the baby to be born, Daddy came back to the old home place and stayed until after the baby was born on July 8, 1924. Our first child was a son, named Davis Haynes Williams. We chose his middle name after our state overseer, Reverend M. S. Haynes.

During this time we still did not have a church, but Daddy preached here and there at various churches in Mississippi. Once while traveling to a meeting in the Mississippi Delta near the city of Cleveland, Daddy decided that he would teach me how to drive. I had never before driven a car, so it was very new to me. I climbed behind the steering wheel and followed Daddy's instructions. However, I soon turned a curve too fast and we lost a tire off of the car.

I remember that I scared Daddy so badly until he was praying for his life. Later, I was driving and managed to clear out a ditch along the roadside. After that, Daddy decided that I really did not need to drive a car as long as he was with me. So, my driving lessons ended promptly. I never drove again until after we retired from the ministry. My son, Davis, then lived in Columbia, Mississippi, and insisted on teaching me how to drive. After I ran over the curb in front of his house, he changed his mind, and, instead, he went out and bought me a little card that read "Back Seat Driver's License."

I also remember that during this time we had a state overseer who did not even live in Mississippi. Brother E. B. Culpepper lived in Georgia and would come over into Mississippi and do what work he could. At that time there were very few people who had cars. The overseer was riding in a spring-seated wagon and ran into a hole in the road. He fell out of the wagon and hurt himself pretty badly. He came on to the place where we were evangelizing near Cleveland, Mississippi. As we were all sitting around the dining room table, I was jesting with him and commented, "Brother Culpepper, people in Mississippi said they'd like to have a state overseer who could ride in a wagon without falling out." He did not like that too well, however, and remarked, "I don't care if they get one that can ride a duck!" We all laughed.

After Davis was born Daddy and I stayed at Vardaman for several months and evangelized throughout the state. Then we learned that a church had come open in Memphis and we were supposed to get it. So, we loaded up what little we owned and went to Memphis in November of 1924. But when we got there we were surprised. It did not work out as we thought. Back then we had state overseers in the Church of God, but they did not help in relocating ministers like they do today. No one really advised you in what to do and what not to do. Well, there was a home preacher that lived in Memphis and when we got there he had taken the church over. So we were still without a church.

Daddy and I had some friends in Memphis that we stayed with for a few days. Then we learned about a church in Ripley, Tennessee, that had come open. We went up there to pastor. We found that they had no church and no parsonage only a brush arbor, so we held meetings in the brush arbor during the summer and rented a hall with sawdust floors during the winter. We had some wonderful services at this church. As usual, I taught Sunday school, played the organ for services, and worked with the young people.

Daddy served as district overseer for the Memphis district while we pastored at Ripley. We often traveled to the various churches and held meetings in communities where Church of God members lived but had no church to attend. We did what we could to strengthen the churches on the district. One of our first duties was to revive the church at Kenton, Tennessee. It was only a few years old and had recently disbanded. We held a meeting in the community and encouraged the people. The Lord blessed us and before the meeting was over a new pastor had been supplied and the church was eager to move forward for the Lord.

During the pastorate at Ripley our daughter Maxine was born on August 31, 1925. She often said that she was a "little Moses" because I kept her hid for three months after she was born. Actually, I just kept her hid from Mama and Papa. I had such a difficult time during my first pregnancy, and I could see how upset it made Mama. So, I did not want to upset her any more until after my second child was born. Then, after Maxine arrived I was almost too ashamed to tell Mama that I had hid it from her. So, Mama never knew until we accepted our next pastorate and went to visit Mama while on our way there. I will never forget the look of surprise on her face when she saw me get out of the car holding my three-month-old "Little Moses."

We stayed at Ripley just over a year and then moved to Red Bay, Alabama, in the spring of 1926. There we began pastoring the Oak Grove Church, which was a large church in the area. The Grissom family was prominent in the community and also members of this church. We loved the people at Oak Grove and they loved us. It was a wonderful time and we experienced many wonderful services there as well. Many young people were saved, sanctified, and filled with the Holy Spirit. I continued to teach Sunday school, work with the young people, and play the organ for services. Daddy also served as district overseer for the local churches. There were also several congregations in this area that, like my home church at Taylor, had remained with Brother Tomlinson. Years later they would become known as the Church of God of Prophecy.

I was also in charge of the singing sometimes back in those days. Services were not as sophisticated in many ways as they are today. Typically, most everyone in the congregation came to the choir and sang. Sometimes there were only one or two people left in the congregation. Everyone gathered around the organ and we would sing various hymns and convention songs. If anyone had a selection they waited until a song had ended and then just yelled out the page number. We would all turn to that page and if I could play it then we would sing it. Sometimes if I could not play the song we would sing it anyway. (But I usually knew how to play most all of the songs. Traveling so many different places I learned that my musical gift was a blessing and I was proud that I had learned music in my home at such an early age.) Often people would get so excited during the singing and begin to shout, dance under the power of God, and speak in tongues. I have seen people get the Holy Ghost while singing and praising the Lord during the song service. I have also seen people get healed while they were singing and rejoicing in the Holy Spirit.

As the years progressed, many people brought other musical instruments to the services. There were lots of guitars, tambourines, trumpets and other brass instruments in some of the churches. Everyone just used what talent they had to help in the work of the Lord. I remember that Sister Pearl Adams and her children had a brass band. She was a lady preacher in the Church of God in Mississippi and her husband had passed away. Each of her children played a musical instrument and they traveled throughout the South singing and preaching. They were special favorites at camp meetings, state conventions, and the general assembly.

But do not think that singing was all we did in our church services. That was just the beginning! After the singing we were always ready to hear the preaching of God's Word. Daddy was such a wonderful preacher. I have seen hardened sinners melt under his preaching and run to the altar to be saved. It is the Word of God that we need to strengthen us in our faith. Sometimes we had services in which the power of God was so strong that Daddy did not get a chance to preach. He would say that the Holy Ghost did the preaching that night. But those services were really directed by the Holy Spirit, because Daddy believed in delivering the Word and he loved to preach as much as he loved to breathe.

While Daddy was a good preacher, sometimes I liked to add to the sermon too. Daddy always let me make comments if I wanted.

Every once in a while I felt like he needed a little help in getting his point across. I acquired this habit during our early ministry and it is one that I still find difficult to break, but have learned that most preachers do not appreciate. So, I have learned to keep my thoughts to myself these days. But you do not live one hundred years and not gain some insight into life. I may be old, but the desire to minister is still strong within me.

We stayed about one year at the Oak Grove Church in Red Bay, Alabama. It broke my heart to leave. But back then preachers went to the Assembly and thought they had to change churches every year. Now we did not have to leave Red Bay, but that was just what most preachers did back then. I hated to leave so badly because I really enjoyed our ministry there.

After leaving Red Bay, we moved to Bush, Louisiana, and pastored Sharp's Chapel near Covington. I also worked in this church, teaching Sunday school and leading the young people. On February 24, 1927, our third child was born soon after we moved there. We named this son Flavous, after General Overseer Flavius J. Lee. That was a growing custom in the Church of God during those days for some reason. Another prominent minister in Mississippi, Brother Grady May, also named his son after Brother Lee. (Flavius J. May later became a preacher and worked at the church seminary in Cleveland, Tennessee, for many years.) Sharp's Chapel had produced many ministers, including Wilson Sharp and William Fount Sharp. We stayed there about a year and then moved to Kentwood, Louisiana.

Kentwood was a nice little town and our son Royce was born there on August 31, 1928. Robert and Rene Blackwood visited with us while we were there and they both preached for us. I always liked Brother and Sister Blackwood, and I had grown up knowing Brother Blackwood's family during my early ministry. I admired Sister Blackwood and well remember that she was a talented seamstress. She made her own clothes (and those for her children) and they looked like she bought them in an expensive department store. Once she told me how she was at a church somewhere and opened up her suitcase to dress the children. The local pastor's wife made a remark about their expensive clothing. Sister Blackwood had to explain how she took one of her old dresses and made clothes for the children from her hand-me-downs. I often wished I could have sown like Sister Blackwood did. Daddy and I loved Brother and Sister Blackwood and also thought much of their children. Kate, who was born while they were pastoring in Morgantown, and Mary Elsie and Bob each taught at Lee College, as well as Mary Elsie's husband Lacy Powell.

We had a successful ministry at Kentwood. Daddy did some excellent preaching and I worked with the music and young people. There were many special people at Kentwood that we learned to love. I was saddened to leave this pastorate, but I have often thought about the wonderful times we enjoyed there.

From Kentwood we moved the Mississippi Delta and took the church at Cleveland. It was called Joseph's Chapel and had been established in 1923. The church at Cleveland did not have a parsonage, but Brother Frank Wolfe owned a lot of land with houses. He let sharecroppers live in the houses in exchange for growing and tending to his cotton for him. He allowed us to live in one of the houses. When it was time for people to move into that particular house, he came over one morning and said, "Well Sister Williams, I've come to move you." I said, "Brother Frank, where are we a'going to move?" He said, "Over into my house." And we moved in with the Wolfe family and lived there as one of the family until the Assembly.

During the time that we lived in Cleveland, I remember we had a member who had fallen by the way and into sin. Back in those days it was the custom of the church to send someone to visit the member in question and try to reconcile with him or her. If that did not work, then two or three people would go and visit the member. (This is what the Bible says we are to do.) Finally, if that did not bring reconciliation, the member was called before the church in its regular conference. If he or she did not acknowledge the offense and apologize or offer reconciliation at this point, the member was often dismissed from church membership. There were also licensed Deacons in the Church of God back then. We had a really good deacon at Cleveland. Once when Daddy asked him to go visit a member in question, our deacon said that he could not make the visit. "The pot can't call the kettle black," he told Daddy. I cannot remember what ever happened with the member, but I always thought the deacon had some integrity about him not to cast a stone at someone else if he was guilty of the same sin. Thankfully, the whole church learned that lesson later on, and today we offer more love toward people in their struggles. I know that sometimes we are too tolerant of sin, but at least we do not turn people completely away from the Lord because of insignificant things like we did so many years ago.

We stayed at Cleveland about a year, and then moved to Dixon, Mississippi. We pastored way out in the country at the Rocky Hill Church, which was located about halfway between Philadelphia and Sebastopol, Mississippi. In addition to serving as pastor of the local church, Daddy also served as district overseer for the Philadelphia district.

One incident that I remember there was the great struggle of getting my four children ready for church on Sunday mornings. This was quite a chore. You can imagine how easily the first few had managed to get dirty by the time I finished dressing the last one. Well, one morning we had a time getting ready and were just a little bit late for service. (We never formed a habit of being late—even if we had to go not looking so well.) Brother and Sister Heath, the state overseer and wife, were there that morning. Sister Heath, who never had any children, made a remark about the family's tardiness. Daddy said, "Sister Heath, how many children did you ever raise?" When she said that she had never raised any, he added, "Well that accounts for your promptness at church!" Often in church we would sing that old song, "Everyday will be like Sunday on that shore." I would think to myself, "Lord, I hope it won't be!" because I always had to do some hustling to get my family ready to be at church on time. Now today I notice so many times that maybe just a man and his wife can hardly get to church on time. That is not a good habit to form.

Another child, a son named Charles, was born on September 16, 1931, while we lived at Rocky Hill. We also had some great services there. I played the organ and taught Sunday school at all of the churches we served. Unless I was pregnant I was teaching young people. I did not think it was appropriate to teach the children and young people while I was expecting. But, I never felt like I could leave my church work undone. I supported Daddy in his ministry and was happy to be a mother, but I also knew that God had called me. I found my fulfillment in working with young people, helping with the music, and teaching. I taught Sunday school classes from the juniors and the card class to the adults. Back then most churches did not have separate classrooms like they do today. We would just divide up into groups at different corners of the sanctuary. Also, I had to stay up late at night and study after the children had gone to bed and my chores at home were done. Yet, I loved my work in the church and believe that God used me to help others learn more about Him.

One of the students in my Sunday school class at Rocky Hill Church was Mary Grace Comans. She was just a little girl then, but she later served a great role for the Church of God in Japan. She went there to serve as a teacher for the children of the United States military servicemen stationed in Tokyo. In addition to teaching, she also began holding services in her home for young people where she read the Bible and shared her faith. Her home Bible studies began to increase until she needed assistance. That is when the Church of God missionaries serving in Japan took an interest in her work. As a result, Mary Grace laid the foundation for what would become the largest Church of God congregation in Japan. Although Mary Grace was never an official missionary, her work has had a lasting impact. I have always been pleased to tell people that once I was Mary Grace's Sunday school teacher.

Unfortunately, we did not have women's ministry programs during the early years. Sister Johnie Belle Wood in Texas started the women's ministry for the Church of God in 1929, and Sister Annie Heath started it in Mississippi shortly after that time. But most local churches did not catch on to the idea until the early 1930s. The first women's ministry program I knew of was when we moved to Morgantown after Daddy was appointed state overseer for Mississippi.

Reverend S. J. Heath became the state overseer of Mississippi in 1929 and also began pastoring the churches at Morgantown and nearby Mount Sinai. He became ill and passed away in February 1931. Then Daddy was appointed to serve as the state overseer. He was immediately thrust into the state work, as the major district conventions had been scheduled and Daddy needed to be present to speak at most of them. I accompanied him to most of the first meetings, but I soon felt needed more at home, especially since I had to tend to the young children and was expecting my son Charles. Initially Daddy continued to pastor at Rocky Hill, but he soon discovered that overseer work kept him away from the local church too much. So, we resigned the church at Rocky Hill and Daddy spent most of his time traveling to churches throughout the state. We remained at Dixon until after Charles was born and then moved to Morgantown in the fall of 1931. We lived at Rocky Hill almost three years.

In Morgantown, Daddy did not pastor the local church. Brother Heath's widow, Annie, was also a preacher and served the local churches for a few months. However, she soon decided that she would like to evangelize, so Brother H. Bynum Magee accepted the position as pastor of the local church. He had already been fulfilling the district pastoral duties and some for the local church when the Heaths were traveling throughout the state.

Sister Heath had no children, so she remained at Morgantown and the church allowed her to continue living in the parsonage. Sister Hettie Pearson, a lady evangelist and member of the Morgantown Church, moved in with Sister Heath for a few months following Brother Heath's death. Sister Pearson also traveled with Sister Heath in evangelistic meetings sometimes. Sister Heath was also the first state Young People's Endeavor superintendent for Mississippi, which position she was appointed to following Brother Heath's death. (This is like an early state youth director.)

Sister Heath traveled extensively while conducting revival meetings and in her youth work. Mava Morgan, a young girl from the community who later married Reverend Joe McCoy, often accompanied Sister Heath. She, along with her sister Geneva Morgan, assisted Sister Heath in starting the first statewide young people's activities in Mississippi. Both Mava and Geneva were good writers, and I often used Geneva's plays and skits in churches where Daddy and I pastored. Another young lady who traveled with Sister Heath was Bessie Branson, a young girl from Florida.

We enjoyed living in Morgantown. This was a special place to Daddy and me—and it would only grow dearer as time progressed. This was—and is—a small village in Marion County, Mississippi. Most of the residents are somehow related and the Alexander, Beard, Boyles, Dunaway, Hammond, Morgan, Pearson, Price, Smith, and Thornhill families have always been prominent. (I think we can add Williams to that list today as well.) This is where the Church of God began in southern Mississippi in 1915, and it was the first Pentecostal movement in the area. As a result, Pentecostalism has always had a strong presence there. In fact, the only churches that have survived in Morgantown have been the Church of God, Church of God of Prophecy, and the United Pentecostal Church.

As we moved to this community, I thought about the first time that Daddy and I visited Morgantown with Sister Nell Lovett almost ten years earlier. It was for the state convention, and on our way home Daddy and I became engaged. Now there we were, moving to Morgantown and Daddy was the state overseer.

Serving as state overseer was not a glamorous position back in those days, especially during the Depression years. The economic condition of the country was burdensome to say the least. Most Church of God people were farmers and factory workers. Too, cotton crops were not paying as much as they had been in many places. Of course, Daddy and I sometimes laughed that preachers were so poor to begin with that we could hardly tell there was a Depression going on. There wasn't much money in our churches back then. The churches were supposed to send offerings to help us along, but most of them were struggling and could not send us anything. People were struggling to keep food on their table and trying to find jobs where they could. Very few members in Mississippi paid tithes back in those days. We were not as enlightened back then on the scriptures about paying tithes and how God will bless us for giving Him our first fruits. Many times we would get reports from the churches and maybe there would be a dollar or two; maybe there would be some postage stamps enclosed. Everyone was having a struggle, but the Lord brought us all through. Today we have so much more than we did back then. I just pray that our churches still have a strong love for one another and the power of the Holy Spirit operating in their midst. That has always been the notable characteristics of our churches, and that is what we worked so hard to cultivate in those early days.

During the Great Depression traveling was difficult. Daddy went to churches as he could, but mainly if they were having trouble. He made certain that he found a means to get there then. I remember Daddy taking the train to churches that were having trouble and working hard to keep peace among the members. One church around Eupora was having trouble and almost had a fight in the church during the meeting Daddy was conducting. He never knew what he would face going to the churches. Once he returned and told me that church members had carried guns into the meeting he was trying to conduct. But those were the exceptions rather than the rule.

Many of our people abounded with love and appreciation for Daddy and his ministry. People back then had to suffer a lot for the gospel and for the church, and we still did not have all the answers either.

Our home was quite small as well. It was as big as the local church parsonage in Morgantown, but it was still small for a family of seven. Too, we always had preachers, evangelists, and people in need staying in our home. (That little house has been well maintained and is still standing about one-half mile from where I now live.)

Living conditions were quite different for ministers during our early pastorates. Very rarely were there parsonages. As overseer of Mississippi and in other travels, we usually had to stay wherever we could with people who were workers, mainly farmers. Most of these people did not have much, but they shared whatever they had. If it was nothing else but going home after church and eating milk and bread, they were happy to share and we were thankful to receive. Most importantly, we enjoyed the love and fellowship of the people. We really did not have many so called "well-to-do" people in our Mississippi churches back then, but most were just country people who had to work hard to make a living working on farms. Oh, but we had such love for one another!

Too, we constantly had preachers, evangelists, state overseers, and church leaders visiting in our home—not just when Daddy was overseer but also when we were pastors. That is just the way it was for the early preachers. I would cook and wash for the visitors just like they were part of the family. It was quite different than it is today in most places.

I can remember times in our ministry that we had an older man who stayed with us for prolonged periods of time. He would tell us stories that we knew could not be true, but we listened anyway. He also liked to sit at the dinner table nearest to the plate of biscuits. When someone asked him to pass a biscuit, he would grab it with his hand and toss it in the air. Our children did not like this at all. Once when Daddy and I were away for the afternoon, our guest was trying to tell the children what to do. Our children did not agree with him, especially Flavous. When the guest picked up an empty basket and tossed it at Flavous, this really did not sit well with him. Flavous picked up a piece of kindling and threw it at the guest. It hit him in the head and caused a large knot to swell. Oh the experiences of life as a minister during the Depression years! Of course, parents would not dream of taking in total strangers in this day and age, but in those days we could not afford to tell such people to leave. They absolutely had no place else to go, and we felt that we were obeying the scriptural command to "do unto the least of these."

Hardship did not hinder the blessings of the Lord, however. Mississippi was experiencing a wonderful outpouring of the Holy Ghost during this time. I can remember that the church in Cleveland, Mississippi, had a powerful revival in which about 50 people were filled with the Holy Spirit. There were also many testimonies of divine healing circulating throughout Mississippi as well. Revivals were being reported everywhere, and churches were being organized all the time. It was then that the Church of God was being established in larger cities. Before then most of our churches were in the rural areas. I believe the first city church in Mississippi was established at Hattiesburg in 1931, which was set in order while Daddy was state overseer and he offered some assistance to that work. Brother Earl Brewer was the state evangelist during that time. He conducted several major revivals throughout Mississippi in 1931 and 1932. In fact, just before we moved to Morgantown, Brother Brewer had preached a long meeting there with more than 40 people receiving the Spirit-baptism. He left there and went to Hattiesburg, where he preached out the local church and set it in order with more than 50 charter members. The Hattiesburg congregation produced numerous ministers, including former general overseer and seminary president Cecil B. Knight.

Daddy and I moved to Morgantown about the time the Hattiesburg church was organized. However, Daddy traveled quite a bit during those years. He preached at meetings all over the state, in one place for a few days and then in another place. Sometimes he conducted revivals that lasted for weeks at the same location. He would send me a letter informing me where he was located and how to pray for the meeting. I suppose his address changed more those two years than at any time in his life. I was not able to travel with Daddy as much as I wanted. I had the family to care for and he scarcely had enough money to pay his own way to and from the meetings throughout the state. But I enjoyed the services at

Morgantown when I could not travel with Daddy. Occasionally I was able to attend the services at Mount Sinai as well.

I remember one service at Mount Sinai that occurred shortly after we arrived in Morgantown in 1931. We were having a singing at the church, and it always drew large crowds. Sometimes spectators just came to watch us worship, especially because of the dancing, shouting and speaking in tongues. That was the reason that Arthur "Ott" and Lillie Price went to this particular service. Lillie had rejected the Pentecostal faith for several years, and felt that Church of God people were too fanatical. During the singing, the Spirit of the Lord began to sweep across the sanctuary and people began to be blessed. Some were shouting and dancing in the Holy Spirit, others were speaking in tongues, and some were weeping before the Lord as He refreshed their soul. An altar call was given for those who wished to receive the baptism of the Holy Ghost. Several teenage boys went forward and knelt at the altar, including Aubrey Lentz (the son of Reverend Joe C. Lentz) and Buford Rawls Price, the son of Ott and Lillie. As the boys were praying, several church members gathered around them and began praying for them. Then, Lillie made her way to the altar and knelt behind her son, placing her hand on his back. That night the Lord filled both Rawls and Lillie with the baptism of the Holy Spirit and they began speaking in a language that they did not understand. Lillie was so overcome with the Spirit that she did not speak a word of English for over two weeks. Instead, she spoke in tongues and began writing "God is love" on various items, including the yard fence to her husband's dismay.

Soon afterward the Price family moved to Morgantown and Lillie became a member of the local Church of God. She served as a faithful member until her death in 1992 at the age of 100. Her Christian influence was well known throughout this area, as she would pray with people where ever she felt led—in department stores, hospitals, the post office, etc. Many people testified of having a desire to receive the Spirit-baptism as a result of her witness. And to think that she once thought Pentecostals were too fanatical! Her family has played a vital role in the Church of God at Morgantown, and her daughter Ethel Rials lived as a wonderful Christian example before the people in this area as well. (In fact, Ethel completed her earthly journey just a few weeks ago at age 93. One Sunday morning she told her family that she was going home. When questioned as to where, Ethel said, "My heavenly home." She then said that the room was full of angels, and a few minutes later Ethel took her last breath. What a testimony, and what a hope! One day the angels of heaven will escort me also from this life into the glory of eternity. We can all have that blessed assurance if we have surrendered our life to the Lord Jesus Christ.)

In 1932 Brother Fount Sharp came to pastor the churches at Morgantown and Mount Sinai. (He was from the Sharp's Chapel Church in Louisiana and in 1929 had completed the church's Bible Training School in Tennessee. While attending BTS he also served as a pastor, including the Mount Olive Church in rural Bradley County near Cleveland.) The church at Morgantown experienced a powerful revival during Brother Sharp's ministry there.

While we lived in Morgantown, we became well acquainted with Reverend Rufus R. Walker and his wife, Leedie. Brother Walker lived in Morgantown and served as principal and coach at the local school. He also pastored the Holly Springs and White Bluff Baptist churches located out in the country from Morgantown. Shortly after Daddy was no longer state overseer and we left Morgantown, a great seven-week revival transpired in the local church in the spring of 1933. Brother James R. Smith, a local evangelist, did some of the preaching, but Pastor Sharp did most of the preaching. During this revival many young people from the school were saved, sanctified, and filled with the Holy Ghost. Watching the impact this had on the students' conduct at school, Brother and Sister Walker began to realize that there was something to the baptism of the Holy Spirit. Too, the Church of God people worked in unity with the Walkers at the school and often let Brother Walker lead testimony service when the Baptist churches were not holding services. Finally, Brother and Sister Walker were convinced that sanctification and the baptism of the Holy Ghost were biblical experiences and they began to pray and cry in the altar to receive the blessing. I was told that the night Brother Walker received the Holy Ghost and began speaking in tongues, he spent hours shouting and dancing in the altar. His white shirt had turned brown from all of the seeking he had been doing on the hardwood floor. When Sister Walker received the Holy Ghost she shouted and worshiped the Lord. She had once remarked that she did not see the need for anyone to scream like one woman (Sister Becky Powell) did in the church, but that is just what Sister Walker did when the Holy Spirit moved upon her. They joined the local church during that revival.

The local school board decided not to renew Brother Walker's contract as principal. Leaders from the Church of God then came to Morgantown and asked him to move to Cleveland and teach at the Bible Training School. Brother Walker accepted and was the first minister in the Church of God with a bachelor's degree. He later served as pastor of the noted North Cleveland Church, a state overseer, superintendent of the orphanage, and General Secretary and Treasurer. That was a powerful revival, not just because of the impact it had on Brother and Sister Walker but because of all the young people who were saved. Ralph Boyles, a well-respected preacher, was also among those whose life was changed as a result of this meeting.

Following the General Assembly in 1932, Daddy's tenure as state overseer ended. We left Morgantown and went back into pastoring. That would be one of the last times that I would have to spend with Sister Heath. About a year later she also left Morgantown, after having been asked to teach piano at the Bible Training School in Cleveland, Tennessee. I remember her to be a wonderful songwriter, often writing songs with Brother M.S. Lemons. (We still sing her song "Heaven's Bells are Ringing" at the local church in Morgantown.) She was also a favorite pianist at the general assembly. While moving to Cleveland, she stopped in Montgomery, Alabama, to preach a camp meeting. She passed away during that meeting. Despite the fact that Sister Heath had corrected me about being tardy for church when we pastored Rocky Hill, I loved Sister Heath and had enjoyed living near her in Morgantown. It saddened me to learn of her passing, but at the time I could only think of the beautiful music that she must be making in Heaven.

We left Morgantown following the Assembly in 1932. As we moved out, Brother T. M. McClendon moved into the community as the new state overseer. However, he soon relocated to Hattiesburg. After leaving Morgantown, we moved to the Mississippi Delta and began planting a church in the City of Greenville. This was one of the earliest Church of God congregations to be organized in a city in Mississippi. In fact, I believe that it was second only to the

Hattiesburg Church. Daddy and I planted this church following the general assembly in 1932. When we started the ministry there, we had to meet in a ball field. That is where we organized the church too. There was no parsonage. We had to share a home with another person and our children had to stay with other people. This was not an easy task for us, but the Spirit of the Lord was heavy upon Daddy and me about planting this church. Since then, the Greenville Church has been one of the strongest congregations in the Church of God in Mississippi.

Around this time, Daddy and I were on our way to a revival meeting and decided to stop for the night in Artesia, Mississippi, and stay with Doctor Daniel and Sister Lou Lamb. (Sister Lou Lamb is one of the early women preachers that I traveled with before my marriage.) When we got there we learned that Doctor Lamb was out on a call somewhere and would not get back until the next day. We found Sister Lou Lamb in an awful shape. She was in severe pain and bedridden. It looked like she was going to die. We gathered together and began to pray for her. We did not get any rest that night because we were praying and interceding for Sister Lamb. The Lambs had a daughter named Mary who was backslidden at the time and off in another room. Sometime during the night Mary came into the room and made things right with the Lord and with her mother. It was only after that happened that the Lord healed Sister Lamb. Doctor Lamb came in the next day and discovered what had happened. It was certainly an amazing event. I have seen the power of God do many wonderful things and I have never forgotten Sister Lamb's healing. She really was at the point of death and then God delivered her. Doctor Lamb was not a member of the Church of God then, although he did not object to it nor did he object to Sister Lamb's ministry. In fact, it was Sister Lamb who led her husband to the Lord. Eventually, that little girl who reconciled herself to God and to her mother became better known as Mary Graves, who served as a Church of God preacher and church planter in Wyoming. As for Sister Lamb, she continued to pastor a church and preach weekly at a local train depot. She witnessed to countless individuals for the rest of her life, and I believe she was over eighty years old when she passed away.

In late 1933 we moved from Greenville and accepted the pastorate at Charleston, Mississippi. This was in Tallahatchie County, where the Church of God first started in Mississippi. There were many wonderful people living in Charleston and the surrounding communities, including several members of the Church of God of Prophecy. Daddy and I often enjoyed visiting with many friends that we had made before the division in the Church of God about ten years earlier.

We stayed at Charleston about a year and then moved to War, West Virginia, where we pastored for five years. This church was located in the mountains. We had never lived in the mountains and it was quite an adjustment for me. One day the former pastor came by for a visit, during which time he asked, "Sister Williams, how do you like the mountains?" I brashly replied, "If God will forgive me for living here one year He won't catch me here the next!" But we stayed there five years and were voted to go back. We had a wonderful pastorate at War and our last three children were born there. Howard was born on March 29, 1934. Darius was born on August 11, 1936, and our baby girl, June, was born on June 28, 1938.

It was tough living away from relatives, especially when they were growing older. But I knew that God had called me, and He gave me grace to be away from those I loved so much. I tried to go home as often as I could, but that was not very much. I remember when I received the news that Papa was ill and wanting to see me. I had prayed with Papa several times, but I was always concerned about his soul. When I learned that he was near death I quickly returned to the old home place. The day after I arrived I could tell that Papa was about to die. I climbed up into the bed with him, prayed with him, and told him to pray. He passed away that day (July 31, 1932) and I was still in the bed with him when he died. I thought about the time I left for ministry and Papa had told me that if I went I "need not come back" home. It had been a long journey and I had traveled many miles since then. But just as he did when I returned from that summer of revival meetings, Papa always welcomed me home. He had then when he was ill, and I am also looking for him to when I get to Heaven.

After Papa died Mama did not have to be alone. Tilmon, my youngest brother, was born later in my parent's life. So he was able to help Mama on the farm. I often wondered what Mama would have done without Tilmon. But when he was about sixteen I received word that Mama was ill. We were still pastoring in War, West Virginia. When I got the word, we had to make arrangements to leave and then we could only drive about thirty miles per hour on the highway. It took us two days and a night to get back to Vardaman. We drove up to a filling station where I knew the man that worked there. I asked him, "Do you know how my mama is?" He looked at me for a second and then solemnly told me, "She was buried yesterday." I broke down and cried there at the filling station. I had so much wanted to make it home before Mama died. We went on to the house where some of the family was waiting on us and then we went to the cemetery to visit the gravesite.

I was thankful that my younger sister, Rena Winters, and her daughter had been able to care for Mama and Tilmon. They had left their home and moved to the old home place to be there for Mama, who died on September 9, 1934.

After spending some time with the family we got ready to leave for West Virginia. When we walked out to load the car, there stood Tilmon with his bags packed. He wanted to go and live with us. There was the 160-acre farm with the house, cows, and good land, but Tilmon did not want to stay. Instead he walked off and left every bit of that to live with us. They rented the house for a while but the renters let the house burn down and then my youngest brother, Tommy Lee Parker, bought all of the land. Tilmon never did return to Mississippi to live. He stayed with us until we left the church at War, West Virginia, and then he went into the service. He later married and retired from the service in Louisiana. About the last time Tilmon visited me, as soon as he walked through the door he hugged me and said, "Mamie, you are more like my mama than anybody." You would have never known but what he belonged to me as far as giving me any trouble or him and the boys getting along. To them he was just like their big brother.

An adventure that our son Charles had at War turned out to be a miracle for us. Daddy and I were away visiting church members and, as usual, left the children at the house. A huge rainstorm had passed through the area, and the creek behind our house began to rise. The creek was at flood stage with trash, limbs, logs, and other things floating downstream. The water was very swift, so Charles decided to turn his wagon into a boat and sail down the creek. The current was so swift that it quickly carried Charles away. Had it not been for the grace of God and our two oldest boys, Davis and Flavous, seeing what had happened, Charles would have most likely drowned. Davis and Flavous jumped in the water and rescued Charles from the rushing water. How grateful we were to God and our other children that they had rescued Charles, whose main concern was that he had lost one of his shoes in the whole ordeal.

While pastoring at War we had a girl in our church in her twenties named Pearl. She did not have any people there except for some distant relatives and she needed somewhere to stay and we needed some help. So, she came and stayed in our home and helped me do my work and tend to the children. Daddy would pay her what he thought he could pay her. Sometimes it would be a little more and sometimes a little less—but it was always a very little. While we were there a Filipino boy, Aurelio Tioaquen, came to stay with us also. He was a student at the Bible Training School and when the term ended he did not have any place to go and somehow he came to live with us. He worked at any job he could get in the community and became just like one of the family. He was a great help to me with the younger children as well.

Two other Bible school students also moved in with us while they were evangelizing in West Virginia following the closing of one of the Bible School terms. They were Mava Morgan from Mississippi and Ora Mae Ruff from Texas. Mava was from Morgantown and knew us quite well. Her family was very active in the local Church of God and community there. She contacted Daddy to see if she and Ora Mae might be able to hold meetings in West Virginia. We opened up our home to them while they were in the state and did not have meetings. Ora Mae had a car that she and Mava traveled in. Charles was just a little boy, but he had decided that he was going to marry Ora Mae because she had a car. He told us that he was going to marry her because she would make him banana pudding and because he could drive her car.

Despite the fact that I was first uncomfortable with the area, I learned to love our time at War. It was a wonderful church with a great spirit of love and powerful worship. It was also nice to finally stay somewhere for more than just a year or two! I believe most all of our family enjoyed those years. We have often laughed at our son Howard, who after getting older tried to impress his school friends by telling them that his dad was "General" and he was born in War!

After five years at War, we received the church vote to return, but Daddy felt like it was time to move to another church. In 1938 we accepted the pastorate at East Rainelle, West Virginia, which had only been organized for a few years. We thought we would really like it there, but soon after we arrived the state overseer began talking with Daddy about the church at Beckley. The church at Beckley wanted to change pastors, and the state overseer felt that a church switch was the answer. We had only been at East Rainelle for a few weeks and had just met most of the members. We really did not want to move, but we prayed about it. Finally, we decided that maybe this was the Lord's will and felt it best to follow the advice of the state overseer. One Sunday the state overseer visited with us. While we were eating dinner, Daddy told him that we had decided to move to Beckley. "Well the Lord don't make you," the state overseer exclaimed. "He just makes you willing!" It was sad to leave those good people at East Rainelle, and I often wondered just how they felt about us staying only a short time.

It was cold weather when we had to move to Beckley. Daddy helped the other pastor and family move their things before he was able to move our things to Beckley. It was Christmas Eve in 1938 when we arrived. The state headquarters was supposed to send us some money to help us out through the holidays, but it did not come in. Daddy and I were concerned about how we were going to make it, and we began to pray and trust God to meet our need. My brother Tilmon was supposed to be visiting with us for Christmas also. Daddy and I did not talk about church problems around our children or relatives. Instead, we joined together in prayer and talked to God about it all. We did not want Tilmon to know about all of the difficulty we had in our move, which had depleted our finances. We did not even have Christmas gifts for the children or food to prepare a special meal. Tilmon arrived in the evening on Christmas Eve and most of our belongings were still packed. We only unloaded the essentials and were camping out in the parsonage for the most part. Daddy decided that we would let Tilmon sleep late on Christmas Day and we would try to figure out what to do. We both prayed that night for God to show us a way to have a special Christmas for the children, especially because the moving was not easy on them.

Shortly after we awoke the next morning, we discovered that the Lord answered our prayer. An older man drove into our yard with a truckload of pounding for us—all kinds of food, including live chickens, and even gifts for the children. Although this man's wife attended the Church of God, he was not even a member of the church! We also enjoyed eggs from those chickens for several months. We had such a wonderful Christmas that year, and it was one of the last that I would share with Tilmon for a long time.

One incident that happened at Beckley has brought us much laughter through the years. Daddy and I were visiting with church members there who were financially well off. This family had a large wood heater with glass doors. It stood several feet high and resembled a clothes dresser. Our son Flavous was with us on this visit and he had never seen a wood heater such as this before. We only had a pot-bellied stove at our house. Flavous, in his childish concern, exclaimed, "Mama, look! That man has a fire in his dresser!" Of course we all laughed then and have laughed even more since.

The Philips family was especially close to us when we lived in West Virginia. In fact, they really became smitten with our son Charles. He had asthma and most everyone made over him because of it, especially the Philips family. They had four daughters but did not have a son. So they took Charles and treated him like he was their little boy. They had horses and Charles liked that, and the girls made a lot over him. When we were leaving, the Philips family wanted to keep Charles, who was about 12 years old. I do not know if I ever could have left him. It would have certainly been the most difficult thing I had ever done in my life, even though I knew that the Philips family was financially able to care for Charles. We told Charles that he would have to make up his mind what he wanted to do. He studied about it for a while and then came and told us, "I want to go with y'all." Of course, I was relieved. You know, a mother is very protective of her children.

We had some wonderful services at Beckley, and the people were very kind to us. I remember those years with much fondness. We stayed at Beckley for almost two years and then moved to South Carolina to pastor the church at Langley. Actually, we lived in Augusta, Georgia, just across the state line from Langley, since there was no parsonage at our new church. It was a good church but the previous pastor was an older preacher who had just retired. He was about the only preacher that this church had ever had. He remained in the congregation after he retired and everyone referred to him as

"Daddy." Brother Williams had a difficult time there. It was not easy trying to get the church settled and everyone's mind off of the former pastor. It was also difficult for the former pastor to give up his role in the church. So, our ministry was not as fruitful at Langley as at other places, but it was a wonderful church. I worked with the youth and women's ministries while we served there. Too, since they did not have a parsonage, we built one while we were there.

We stayed at Langley for one year before moving to Walhalla, South Carolina. We had a wonderful experience there and stayed for two years. It was there that Daddy personally purchased some furniture for the parsonage. We had a nice dining table and wood stove, as well as our own bedding. As usual, I had canned up a lot of stuff and we lived off of that during the winter. (Mama had taught me well!) Daddy had a truck that we could move more things when we went to leave, but there was still little room to take much with us. So, when we moved we left the church some nice furniture and lots of canned food. I used to laugh and say that at least the next pastor's family surely slept well and did not go hungry! But it really was a wonderful church and we learned to love the people so much. I enjoyed our ministry at Walhalla as much as I did anywhere. We had a great revival while we were there with many people accepting Christ and being filled with the Holy Spirit. The Lord really blessed the church and us while we were there. Many times I wished we had stayed there.

Our children really loved it at Walhalla as well. They all had friends and enjoyed the freedom of the community. Sometimes they enjoyed that freedom a little too much. Once our son Flavous was going to play with some of his friends following dinner one evening. Daddy told him what time the door would be locked that night. Well, Flavous was not home when Daddy locked the door and we all went to bed. The next morning we found Flavous. He was sleeping with the dog on some hay under our back porch! That taught him a valuable lesson about being home on time.

We also taught our children to be at the dinner table on time, and they were pretty good about doing that. We never went to the table without thanking the Lord for His blessings and asking Him to bless our food. We also had family prayer time every evening. We all gathered together and listened to Daddy read from the Scriptures, and then we said our evening prayers together. Our children were not perfect, and now I think that we were sometimes too strict on them. But, it is not easy being a pastor and having everyone watch your family. Often when we moved into a new community, the neighborhood children tested our boys. I have tended to many scrapes and bruises as a result. Sometimes I think about it and see how we could have done differently in raising our children, but Daddy and I always loved them and tried to train them up to serve the Lord.

From Walhalla we moved to Michigan to pastor the North Woodville Church of God near Big Rapids, Michigan. This was during World War Two. This was a difficult move for us. We had been informed that people in Michigan were not friendly, and the children were grieved at this thought. It was Maxine's senior year of high school, and she was saddened to think of spending her last year of school with people who were unfriendly. As was his custom, Daddy went with the children on their first day of moving to a new school. He met with the teachers and got a sense of what the school and teachers were like. The whole family, especially Maxine, was surprised to discover that the teachers and students were so friendly. In fact, students often gathered around Maxine and asked her questions. The teacher often called on her to answer questions in class. We later learned that they were fascinated with our southern accent and enjoyed listening to us talk!

However, that was not the only surprise we experienced in Michigan. One of the church leaders had recommended the church to Daddy and told him what it paid. He asked Daddy if he thought we could live on that. Daddy felt like we would be able to get by, but we were badly deceived. Daddy trusted this leader and considered him a friend from their early ministry together, but when we moved there we found the situation was not as we had been told. We had a very difficult time financially, and were quite a large family.

Davis went into the service and Daddy and Flavous went to work at Gerber's Food Market. We stayed at the Big Rapids Church about as long as we could, but Daddy realized that he was going to have to move into town to get a better job in order to support the family. We had to leave the church because it was not a supporting church and we just could not make it financially. We were only there for about six months.

Daddy found a church to pastor at Inkster, near Detroit. The parsonage there was not large enough for the family, so the children and I stayed near Big Rapids, where we attended the local

Church of God. Sometimes Maxine attended the Baptist church with several of her close school friends. Of course, Daddy and I always felt that Baptists were Christians too, so this did not worry me too much. However, Daddy did not like being away from the family, nor did we like being away from him.

This was during World War Two and Davis had enlisted in military service. He was serving overseas in the United States Navy. I still remember the heartache I felt as I watched Davis leave us. I wondered if I would ever see him again, but I was determined to pray and fast until the Lord brought him safely back to me. I practically stayed on my knees in prayer. Later I learned that his ship had been hit during a major battle near Japan. All of the sailors were forced overboard into the water. Davis watched as sharks pulled his crewmates under the water to their deaths. All around him people were dying, but the Lord spared Davis from the sharks and kept him safe until the rescue ship arrived. Both Flavous and Royce also served in the Navy, but, thankfully, they never had to fight in any battles overseas. I was so happy to see my boys return home from that war.

It was also while we lived in Michigan that Maxine met R. C. Edwards. He had moved to Michigan to work in the oil fields there. R. C. and Maxine were soon married and raised a family of three children: Bob, Joyce, and Linda. Today they live in Texas.

The family was still having a great financial struggle, and Daddy was under a great deal of strain. It was becoming too much for us. Finally Daddy saw that he was going to have to find full-time secular work to provide for the family. So, we moved into the city of Dearborn and Daddy got a job in the oil field working on land. At this time Daddy did not have a church, but we were attending the local Church of God. It was about all Daddy could do to hold down the job and keep the family fed. One day the church leader who had recommended the previous church to us came by our house. Daddy was working, but I was home with the rest of the family. I sat down and visited with the minister about our experience at the last church and how Daddy had to get a better job to support us. I was shocked when this minister looked at me and asked, "Doesn't Brother Williams realize this is going to hurt him in the ministry?" That cut deep in my soul and hurt me badly. This minister could have helped Daddy if he would have, but instead I felt like he was pointing a finger at him. I knew how much Daddy loved to minister and how badly he wanted a church to pastor, but for the moment he had a family that needed food on our table. He was doing what he thought he had to at the time. I was terribly hurt by that church leader and it took a long time to get over it.

Several years later we were living in Meadville, Mississippi. Daddy had been pastoring again for quite some time. (He was only out of the pastorate for about one year until we left Michigan and returned to Mississippi.) There was a church meeting in Jackson, Mississippi, and Daddy wanted to go. I knew that this particular church leader was going to be there and really did not want to see him because I was still hurt. Daddy did not feel by this minister like I did, so I finally consented to go with Daddy to the meeting. We walked in the door of the church just before the service started. That minister saw us enter the sanctuary and walked from the pulpit and met us halfway down the aisle. As he approached us that feeling of hurt left me just like a bird flying up in the air. I believe that is the greatest experience I have ever had with forgiveness. It did not matter anymore what wrong had been done to us. I realized that this minister was my brother in the Lord. Nothing was ever said about the past, the Lord just took the feeling away and restored my love for this preacher. That night I realized that sometimes we harbor hurt by not choosing to forgive. Daddy and I were not serving that particular preacher; we were serving Jesus. And Jesus had never failed us!

In fact, that time Daddy spent working a secular job was perhaps one of the greatest blessings for our life after retirement, but we had no idea of its importance at the time. We saw it as a difficult trial when we were going through it, but years later we realized that God was looking out for us and working all things for our good the whole time. Daddy paid into Social Security while working that job, so when he retired we were able to draw from that Social Security and it was a great help for our retirement income. In fact, I am still reaping the benefits even today.

Daddy also saw that during that time of secular work he was able to see the other side of life. Having been totally involved in the ministry since he was sixteen, Daddy had never had to work so closely with those who were not Christians. This actually helped him to understand people better, and I believe it helped him become even more effective as a minister.

Now I must say that life was not void of joy in Michigan. We made many wonderful friends while we were there. At Dearborn, we even paid some down on a home. Daddy and I considered retiring there, and we had some good church friends there. But, we soon got a desire to return to Mississippi and eventually left Michigan in 1946.

Upon our return to Mississippi, Daddy accepted the pastorate of the Church of God at Crystal Springs. This was a small congregation and holiness was not well accepted in this town. Most in the community were determined that they did not want another Pentecostal church, and they worked against the church in many ways. It was still difficult for us, but Daddy was so happy to be pastoring again.

Our son Davis married while we were pastoring at Crystal Springs. He was working with the Navy and met his wife, Lavern Stewart, while he was stationed in Jackson, Mississippi. Lavern was originally from Kokomo, Mississippi—a rural community near Columbia. Davis and Lavern married and had two children of their own, Carolyn and Larry, and also adopted their nieces, Sandy and Pam. They lived in various places, but retired in Columbia, Mississippi.

We stayed at Crystal Springs about a year and then returned to Morgantown, Mississippi in early 1947. This time Daddy pastored the local church. When we moved there we had a small, unfurnished parsonage and Daddy purchased furnishings on his own. He paid on it weekly as he had help. Today there is a nice brick parsonage, and I am so glad for it. And, I am thankful that it is furnished nicely. I have no jealousy and no envy about our ministers living better today than we were able to. It was just part of the persecution of the time in which we lived—the beginning of preaching the Pentecostal blessing in Mississippi and other places.

However, we found that Morgantown was not out-dated. Actually, it was different than when we had last lived there. Instead of the white frame building there was a nice brick building, the results of a mighty revival in 1945 that had last lasted for nine weeks. This was during the pastorate of Reverend William R. Messer, whom we followed. As for the revival, it began when Opal Morgan, a young lady in the church, received the Holy Ghost while visiting relatives, Joe and Mava McCoy, in Dillon, South Carolina. When she returned and testified of her experience, the community was stirred. People began to receive the Holy Ghost, young and old alike. Then, Sister Effie Dunaway, a minister's wife who had been a cripple for seven years, was instantly healed in a service during the revival. That really stirred the community. The new church building was constructed in 1945 and it was the first brick building in the Church of God in Mississippi. It was the most up-to-date facility in Mississippi and cost $8,500. My how times change!

When we arrived in 1947, we found that the people were still hungry for the Lord. The Second World War was still fresh on our minds, although it had ended two years prior. But spiritual fire was still burning in the hearts of the people at Morgantown. Shortly after we arrived, Daddy began to see wonderful results to his preaching. We had a seven-week revival in the spring of 1947 with Brother Earl Brewer of Hattiesburg preaching four of those weeks. Young couples began to get saved, sanctified, and baptized with the Holy Ghost. Several people were also healed, including Ruby Lee Morgan. She was healed of sugar diabetes and was also filled with the Holy Ghost and joined the church during this meeting. She and her husband, Sidney Morgan, both became workers in the local church for many decades before moving to the Mississippi Gulf Coast and working in the Church of God at Gulfport. Also, Jay Bracey was saved in this revival. His wife, Hazel Hammond Bracey, had joined the local church as a charter member when she was twelve years old. However, Jay was not one to attend church, but the Lord did touch his life during that revival.

We saw the indebtness of the church paid off while we were at Morgantown, too. In 1945 Joe and Mava McCoy had given the first one hundred dollars for the new building. During the seven-week revival in 1947, Eddie Heck paid the final one hundred dollars. Brother Heck was a member of the Church of God Melody Boys Trio from the Shepherd's Fold Church in Covington, Louisiana. Another member of the group had been raised in Morgantown and was the son of Freddie and Annie Belle Alexander. Sister Annie Belle was a prominent pastor and evangelist in the Church of God in Mississippi and Louisiana. She and Brother Freddie lived in Morgantown when they were not pastoring. After the indebtness was paid, the church decided to build new Sunday school rooms onto the church. This proved to be a great blessing to the church and a boost for the Sunday school program, as they needed extra space. Years later I taught a women's Sunday school class in one of those rooms.

We left Morgantown in 1949 with a sense of great accomplishment. The Lord had done many wonderful things while we were there. Most of all, many sinners had found the love of Jesus and many Christians had received deeper experiences with the Lord through the Holy Spirit. Yet, it would not be our last journey through Morgantown.

Our next pastorate was at Byrd's Chapel Church of God near Meadville, Mississippi. This was an area where Daddy had a fruitful ministry before our marriage. He knew many of the people in Meadville and the surrounding towns of Bude, McCall Creek, and Natchez.

We held services in a church building that had long served the congregation. It had a tin roof, cracks in the floor, and wooden benches. Many of our older churches throughout the Church of God at that time had buildings much the same. But Daddy and I always desired to leave a church better than we had found it, and Byrd's Chapel was no exception. One day a storm swept across the area and blew down much of the timber. The company that owned the land on which the timber had been standing gave the logs to church people. With our portion of the timber we began constructing a new church. A new, brick building was erected, along with Sunday school rooms and a basement. We also added on to the parsonage, including providing indoor plumbing and a bathroom. The congregation was so proud of the new church, and we were too.

It seemed that most of our family scattered during our pastorate at Byrd's Chapel. Darius went to college in Hattiesburg, Mississippi, during the week. He also met his wife, Brenda Holland, during this time. She and her family were prominent members in the local church. Her sister, Bonnie, also played the piano for most of our services. I assisted with the music when I was needed, but I spent most of my time working with the youth and women's ministry. Darius and Brenda married and have spent most of their life together in Baton Rouge, Louisiana, and Meadville, Mississippi. They had three children: Kim, Gregory, and Dara.

Flavous also married while we were pastoring at Byrd's Chapel. His wife, Ann Stringfield, was from Morgantown and the granddaughter of Sister Clara Priest, one of the earliest women preachers in the Church of God. Flavous and Ann married in 1953 and lived in Louisiana before returning to Morgantown in the mid 1960s. They have three children: Becky, Martha, and James "Bo."

Royce met his wife, Elizabeth Bates, at Byrd's Chapel as well. Elizabeth was a local girl, and she and Royce have three children: Dale, Donna, and Darrel. Royce and Elizabeth have spent most of their life in Fernwood, Mississippi.

Charles also married while we were living at Byrd's Chapel. He had met Voncil Morgan while living in Morgantown. Her mother was Dolly Morgan, who had been an early member of the Church of God in Morgantown. Charles and Voncil have two sons, Van and Don. They lived most of their life in Laurel, Mississippi, but now live near me in Morgantown.

Our ministry at Byrd's Chapel was very special to us. Despite the hardship we had suffered several years previous, God had proven Himself faithful yet again. Our service to the Lord and to the church after returning to Mississippi was very refreshing to us. Oh yes, there were still struggles as with all life, but the blessings were so abundant that we were continually thankful for God's provision.

While we lived at Byrd's Chapel our son-in-law, R. C. Edwards, was called into military duty. He had previously served in World War Two as well. Our son Charles had just completed high school, so he went to live with Maxine in Texas for two years while R. C. was away in service. I can remember thinking that my "nest" of children was quickly becoming empty.

We had several wonderful revivals while at Byrd's Chapel. One of the first revivals that Brother Paul Henson preached after he and Geri Humphries were married was for us at Byrd's Chapel Church. Paul and Geri were just teenagers, but he tried to be a little man. He was certainly a good preacher. They stayed in our home with us. I think Brother Henson brought back many memories to Daddy of his early days as a teenage preacher roaming through those nearby woods to preach to the spiritually hungry. Daddy certainly loved Brother and Sister Henson, and my kids and I still do. Brother Henson has served the Church of God in many positions, including as the state youth director of Mississippi. He recently served as director of SpiritCare, which helps take care of all of the retired pastors and spouses in the church. Yes, I am now one of those and am thankful for everything the Church of God does for me.

I well remember one of the revivals with Brother Henson. Various people in the church were given a specific hour to pray. We would wake up at whatever time we had been given and pray for the meeting, especially for sinners and backsliders to come to a personal relationship with Jesus Christ. And, of course, all of the church was asked to participate in days of fasting. Oh, did we have a good meeting! I still believe that fasting and intercession are keys to revival. We need more of it in the church today.

Another young minister who conducted a successful revival for us at Byrd's Chapel was Brother Paul Barker. He was just a schoolboy from the Midwest. He found his way to Mississippi after Reverend E. R. Waller followed us as pastor of the Morgantown Church. (Brother Waller had served as the state youth director in the Midwest before moving to Mississippi.) Brother Barker conducted a revival in Morgantown that continued so long until he enrolled in the high school there. After finishing that meeting, he came to Byrd's Chapel and conducted a meeting for us.

We had a mighty good time worshiping the Lord during that revival as well. Brother Barker stayed in our home, as was the custom of our evangelists. He ate with us and I cleaned his clothes for him. I especially remember that at that time he only had one suit, which was natural for a young boy his age. I washed it and pressed it for him each day before service in the evening. Then I decided to provide him with a pounding of clothes. With the help of the local women, we gathered several nice clothes. One evening before service we all entered the back door singing "There'll Be Showers of Blessings" and gave him the clothes. I remember how grateful he was. Brother Barker has also served the Church of God in several positions, including state overseer of Nebraska and as pastor of some of our noted congregations. Today he is the pastor at Byrd's Chapel, which is now called Praise Cathedral and the congregation worships in a brand new facility.

We stayed at Byrd's Chapel for five years and then accepted the Church of God at Columbia, Mississippi. We arrived there in January 1955 and many of our members at that time were women. Some of the members that I remember include Ruby Bostwick,

Mamie Kaufman, Louis Bullock, and the Meltons. There were also two lady preachers in our congregation, Sister Lettie Meadows (who had started the local church in her home) and Sister Flora Cooper. We had some wonderful services while pastoring in Columbia. I played the piano, worked with the youth and women, and taught a Sunday school class. We also added Sunday school rooms on to the church during our service there. I wish I knew how many times we made fried pies and sold them to raise money for the building fund!

In September 1956 we left Columbia and moved to McComb, Mississippi. We pastored there for about three years. I continued to work in the church, although I was about to get too old to work with young children. Nonetheless, I did all that I could. I played the musical instruments when I was needed and directed the women's ministry program for the local church. While we were pastoring in McComb we looked for a parsonage because the church did not have one. Daddy and the men of the church spent much time searching for a suitable location. Finally, a house was located that the congregation liked and they purchased it. This was a blessing both to us and to the church.

Our daughter June attended college at Summit, Mississippi, during this time. And she also met her husband during our pastorate at McComb. Reverend Don Clark was an evangelist who held a revival for us while we were there, and he and June were married. They have three children: Randy, Melanie, and Kerry. Don and June have spent over forty years together in the ministry. Currently, they are pastoring with the Church of God in Florida.

Our son Howard also attended college after serving in the military. He went to Daddy's alma mater, Lee College in Cleveland, Tennessee. There he met Linda Tharp from Arkansas. They have four children: Joy, Darla, Stephen, and Perry. Howard and Linda live in Columbia, Mississippi.

After McComb we moved to Dunn, Louisiana, in 1959. This was our last church to pastor, but it was certainly a wonderful experience for us. This church was one of the first congregations for the Church of God in Louisiana, and during our service there it consisted of mostly older people. This was the home church for the Walker family, including Reverend J. Herbert Walker Sr. who had served as the general overseer for the Church of God from 1935 to 1944. Occasionally he visited, and Daddy and I always enjoyed sharing old stories and laughs with him and his wife, Blanche. Brother Walker's sister, Iredell, was one of our most faithful members and my best friend there. Like Daddy, she had attended the Church of God Bible Training School and graduated from there in 1929. Iredell led the choir and I often played the piano, but there was also another girl who could play the piano too. I remember that we had some wonderful singing at the Dunn Church. Several of the members knew music well and we had a good time. I also learned how to play the French Harp (harmonica) while Daddy and I pastored the church at Dunn. The first song I learned to play was "Cotton-Eyed Joe." I still enjoy playing the harmonica today, even at age of 100 plus.

When I look back at all of the places we ministered, I realize just how good God was to us. There was a great fight to make back during the early days of Pentecost, but the Lord helped us to be able to bear and go through with all of the temptations and persecutions that people had back then, especially in Mississippi. The constant moving from community to community and church to church was not always easy, but that was just the custom back in those early days. Preachers thought they had to change churches each time they went to the general assembly. But those days were so full of God's goodness. I am so thankful to the Lord for His protection and blessings through it all. Today my children and I sit around and discuss those old ministerial experiences. We look back and think about the places we lived and people we met. We don't focus on the negative either, but we always talk about the fun and humorous things. Times were not easy, but the good was so much better than the bad!

9

Slowing Our Pace

By 1962 Daddy and I had both reached 60 years of age. I had been serving in active ministry for 43 years, and Daddy had been in active ministry for 45 years. We decided that it was time to retire. So, we resigned our church at Dunn, Louisiana, and returned once again to Morgantown, Mississippi. Several of our children had settled in this area, and we wanted to be near them and our grandchildren. Too, we had many friends in Morgantown and it had always been a special place to us.

We did not know what we would do at first, however. Like so many other preachers, we had no savings, no home, and nowhere to go. Our son Flavous allowed us to rent a home from him that was located near the Church of God. Daddy insisted on paying rent. He got a job driving a school bus back and forth to West Marion School, and soon we were able to purchase the house from our son. Daddy insisted that we do that because he wanted a home of his own. The only other home we had owned was in Dearborn, Michigan, when we thought we were going to retire there. But we did not keep it after we returned to Mississippi. It was very gratifying for us to finally have something that we could call our own.

Daddy decided that he was tired and needed rest, so he proposed that he was retiring from the ministry completely. I was not so sure that his decision would be as final as he proposed, but I was glad that we had finally settled down. We had earned this time together. Daddy soon became restless and accepted occasional weekend preaching engagements at nearby churches and at places where we had pastored. We held services at McComb, Byrd's Chapel, Columbia, two churches in Poplarville, Mississippi (Murray Hill and Mitchell Chapel), and other churches near Morgantown such as Mount Sinai and Mount Carmel. But mostly we worked in the local church at Morgantown.

Brother Ralph Boyles, with his wife Helen, was serving as pastor of the church at Morgantown when we returned. Brother and Sister Boyles were natives of Morgantown, and Daddy and I always thought so much of them. Daddy took an active role in the Men's Bible class taught by Brother Jim Easterling. I began teaching the Ladies' Bible class and served as the teacher for thirteen years. (In 1975, when I was seventy-four years old, I turned the class over to Sister Lorena Gartman, who then served as my Sunday school teacher until her death in 1999.) Some of the members of my class were Annie Belle Alexander, Lillian Morgan Boyles, Flora Morgan Dunaway, Lillie Price Dunaway, Lizzie Evans Dunaway, Nellie Beard Dunaway, Wilda Pearl Freeman, Johnie Williamson Hammond, Julia Beard Hammond, Otelia Hammond (the wife of the local state representative, Kelly J. Hammond), Ella Morgan Johnson, Lavada Morgan, Lena Carney Morgan, Hettie Pearson, Lela Hammond Smith, and Ollie Herrington Sumrall. I remember buying postcards with a pretty scene and the caption, "We Missed You in Sunday School." I mailed these regularly and also made phone calls to those who missed the class. I considered teaching that class just as serious as anything else I had endeavored to do for the Lord. It was a great blessing for me to have the opportunity to have an outlet for my ministry, especially as I advanced in age.

Daddy and I enjoyed our retirement together. As much as we loved the ministry, it was good to have the release and enjoy spending time with each other without the responsibility of seeing after others. It had been 40 years since it was just the two of us, and we enjoyed it!

We spent our days visiting in the community, going into the woods to pick wild berries, and tending to the garden. Daddy always had a garden, but he really enjoyed gardening after we retired. I also enjoyed helping him with it. It was a good outlet for us. In later years Daddy grew tired while working in the garden, so he placed a chair at either end of the rows where he could sit and rest when he felt weary. Occasionally I would yell out the back door to make sure he was okay, and he would let out a yell to let me know he was okay. He had some really big gardens during those years, including one time when we had to climb a ladder to reach the corn.

We also enjoyed going to the post office, which was located in the country store across the road from the church. Feldon "Bud" Morgan owned the store and also served as postmaster. Sometimes our daughter-in-law Ann would be the substitute postmistress. Daddy used to sit and wait on the mail to be put in the boxes and enjoy talking with others who had also gathered. Most of them sat on an old church bench that was against the wall in the store.

Daddy and I went to town quite often as well. That meant that we drove into Columbia, the county seat for Marion County. That was where the courthouse, shopping centers, hospital, and doctors' offices were located. Once when we went to the doctor, Daddy went in first. When I went in to see the doctor he asked, "Well, your husband just told me that he was 'General Grant.' So, who are you?" I answered just a seriously as I could, "Mamie Eisenhower." And then I had to laugh along with the doctor. I am not certain if the doctor ever believed that was Daddy's real name, but it was.

In August of 1973 Daddy and I celebrated our Golden Wedding anniversary. We had a large celebration with our family and friends. There was also a special service in which we renewed our vows to each other. At the time we did not even think about making it to our sixtieth anniversary, but we did. We celebrated that one in 1983. That occasion was a family celebration held nearby in Columbia. In all, Daddy and I were married for almost 66 years.

Our family and the Morgantown community were the main focus of our activities, especially the church. Another pastor that Daddy and I grew very close to was Morgantown's long-term pastor, Brother Tommy Lee Waldon and his wife. Brother Waldon served 11 years (from 1966 to 1977), which is the record for a pastor at Morgantown. Brother Gary L. Baugh and wife Ann followed him. They were a sweet couple.

Brother Dempsey Neese and his wife Lou pastored there next. We had some wonderful singing while Brother Neese and his family were at Morgantown. One humorous thing that I remember was that Brother Neese preached several times about Abraham and Sarah. He talked about how God had given them a child when Sarah was 90 years old. One Sunday morning as Daddy and I walked home from service, I told him, "Well if Brother Neese thinks we are going to be another Abraham and Sarah, he has another think coming!" Then I looked up at Daddy and we both had a good laugh all the way home.

Another humorous event was the night that I decided we needed a bigger bed. It seems that while Daddy was sleeping he dreamed that he was chasing a frog. He finally managed to sneak up on the frog and reached out his hand to catch it. Just as he did that in his dream, he popped his hand across my head. I woke up startled, only to awaken Daddy by my scream. After that, the children purchased a nice king-sized bed for us, which I still sleep on today. The first night that we slept on the new bed, I told Daddy that he could go frog catching all he wanted to—as long as it was on his side of the bed. We both laughed.

And such were our final years together—filled with laughter and remembering how faithful God had been to us through the years. Daddy and I still cared for others and ministered in various personal ways, but we took our retirement years to enjoy being with each other and with our family. I believe we had earned that privilege. We enjoyed life.

10

Learning to Walk Alone

Growing older has many advantages. I have lived long enough to understand many things about life, especially how I could have done some things differently. I have also learned to focus more on the things that are really important. Oh yes, there have been days when I looked in the mirror and clearly saw the wrinkles, white hair (and less hair), and slumped posture. I am reminded that I am 100 years old, but more so these days from all the aches and pains that I feel. My eyesight is now dim, so when I look in the mirror I just imagine myself as I once was—the youthful figure with smooth cheeks and full, dark hair. Yet, age has taught me to appreciate the good things and the good times. They pass by so quickly. Nothing makes that seem more real than losing those you love the most.

I suppose that one of the most difficult things for a mother is to lose her child—that being which she gave birth to and watched grow into a man or woman. When a voice is stilled that often said, "I love you Mother," it creates a pain from somewhere deep within. I experienced that when Daddy and I lost our oldest son, Davis.

Each year my family has a reunion near my old hometown of Vardaman, Mississippi. I have been able to go for many years, even at my advanced age. However, in July 1982 Daddy and I rode with our son Davis to the Parker family reunion. His wife, Lavern, had gone on a church trip, so it was just us on this trip. The first night that we were there, Daddy and I stayed with one of my sisters and Davis stayed with his first cousin. The next day when Davis came to pick us up and take us to the reunion, I noticed that he was coughing badly. As we drove down the road, we planned to stop off at the house of another one of my sisters. Before we got there Davis had a terrible coughing spell. I was sitting in the backseat of the car and offered him some mints, but I do not know if he ever had a chance to take them. When we arrived at my sister's house, I noticed that Davis staggered as he got out of the car. As soon as we entered the house, he went straight to the air vent and held open his shirt. About that time be began to fall backward and Daddy caught him, placing him on a nearby bed. Davis never did leave that bed and died a couple of hours later. Daddy and I were there with him when he took his final breath on July 10, 1982, two days after his 58th birthday. I cannot describe how it feels to watch your child leave the confines of this earth. I had always wanted to protect my children, and Daddy had too. But I sat there helplessly. I prayed and begged the Lord to touch Davis, but his time had come and I had to let him go. That was not an easy thing for Daddy and me to do. It took us several months, and even today I still miss Davis.

Oh, how Daddy and I did grieve! I was very open with my pain and cried for weeks afterward. Daddy would not let me see him grieve. He tried to be strong for me, but sometimes I think it would have helped me to see him grieve more. Daddy eventually accepted Davis's passing, but I still grieved and cried. I did not want to let him go. Finally, Daddy talked with me. I was sitting on the side of my bed looking at a picture of Davis and crying. Daddy came to me and said, "Now mother, you know that D. H. called on the name of the Lord and asked Him to forgive him. You must stop grieving. Grieve no more."

On that day I asked the Lord to touch me, and I decided that I must release my son to Him. I knew that is what Davis would want me to do. And I thought about all of those years that I had told the Lord that He would have to take care of Davis because I was not with him anymore. I had to be willing to give him to the Lord again. And yes, I would see Davis again. I knew that he was a Christian. I remembered the time that he had wanted to join the Baptist church in Columbia, Mississippi, where he and Lavern attended. She was joining the church, but Davis said that he would not join the Baptist church as long as Daddy and I were living. When we found this

Daddy and I were living. When we found this out, Daddy and I went to see Davis and told him that we wanted him to join the church. That is all it took and Davis joined the First Baptist Church in Columbia. He became very active in the church, especially by teaching Sunday school and singing. (He always did love to sing! Also, Lavern has been a great worker in that church ever since she became a member.) I thought about all of that as I sat on the side of my bed, and the Lord began to fill my heart with peace and assurance. While I still miss not having Davis, my soul began its journey to healing that day. Just as He promised, the Lord did not forsake me in that hour of great trial. And He is with me still!

After my wounded spirit began to heal, I became more like my old self. Daddy and I continued to enjoy being with our family and friends. The church was always a part of our lives, and we found strength in attending the services and staying active in its activities. Not long after Davis' death, the Reverend Pettis Brewer and wife Jean moved to Morgantown. I have always thought so much of Brother and Sister Brewer, especially how he spent so much time with Daddy. Brother Brewer would come by our house and visit with us quite often. We talked about our ministry and told him about the many adventures we had while pastoring. Brother Brewer almost seemed like he belonged to us.

As time drifted on, I noticed its affect on me. I could also see how growing older was affecting Daddy. He began to have bad spells where he would lose his breath. Once he blacked out while standing in the post office portion of the community store in Morgantown. But as long as he could go, Daddy drove our little blue car. More and more Daddy began to feel so weak that he could not go to church. I knew that if Daddy did not go to church, then he must be ill. Church has always been such a vital part of our life, and I still do not like to miss the services. I remember one Sunday morning when Daddy was at home because he did not feel like going to church, but he insisted that I go on to service. Sometime during the morning service the back doors of the church opened and I heard a commotion. Then I heard Daddy rejoicing in the Lord and speaking in tongues. I turned to see him shouting down the aisle of the church. The Lord had touched his body and he had made it to church after all. Needless to say, we all had a wonderful time rejoicing in the Lord that day.

There was another time when Daddy had taken ill while we were visiting in Texas with our daughter, Maxine, and her husband,

R. C. Edwards. They attend the Assembly of God church in their community, and Daddy and I went with them to church. Daddy was not feeling well, but he insisted on going to church. He enjoyed visiting with the members there, and they always seemed to make over him. Daddy received a powerful touch from the Lord during that service, and he began walking throughout the sanctuary—up and down the aisles and in between the pews. He was rejoicing in the Lord and moving his arms and legs with all his might. Daddy was claiming his healing, but Maxine was afraid that he was going to work up another weak spell. It was quite a sight to see Daddy rejoicing throughout the church and Maxine running behind him with her arms ready to catch him at any moment. But, the Lord did touch Daddy that day and Maxine just got some good exercise.

Daddy and I always loved to rejoice and bless the name of the Lord. After we retired, we continued to maintain a good prayer life and time of devotion together. We also enjoyed praying with our guests while they were visiting with us. Sometimes we would pray in the family room, at other times we would pray in the bedroom if Daddy was feeling weaker. (His favorite chair was located in our bedroom.) Often we would cry and rejoice at the same time. I have seen the power of God move upon Daddy many times while he was praying, causing him to tremble and weep before the Lord while he spoke in tongues and magnified the name of the Lord. Those are sweet memories.

Eventually Daddy's weak spells became worse. He would lose his breath and I would think that his time had come. But, the children worked with him and made him walk, which helped him regain his breath. This went on for quite a while, but Daddy never slowed down.

One night we went to bed as usual; everything seemed normal. Daddy got up in the middle of the night to go to the bathroom. I woke up when he got out of the bed. Then when he came back to the bedroom, he staggered in the doorway. I jumped out of the bed and ran to him and helped him get to the side of the bed. I thought he must have had another spell, and I offered him a mint. I do not think he ever had a chance to take the mint. I ran to the telephone and called our son Flavous. As I went to the phone, I heard Daddy yell out, "Oh!" just as if he were surprised about something. When Flavous answered the phone, I remember yelling, "Your daddy's dying! Your daddy's dying!" By the time I got back to Daddy, he was no longer breathing. I started praying for him, but I knew the Lord had called him home. I have often thought about that old saying how a Christian walks up and down the Jordan River looking for their place to cross. I guess that night Daddy found his crossing.

In just a few moments' time, I relived thousands of events that Daddy and I had shared in our 65 years of marriage. Through my tears I remembered him sitting next to me at the state convention before we married, then our wedding, then swimming together in the pond at Gloster. I thought about the times I had heard him preach and watched the power of God flow through him to touch so many lives. There he was coming home from a hard days work in Michigan when he had to give up his church just to provide for his family. Then I saw him working in the garden and gathering in that corn while standing on a ladder. I thought about our fun times with our children and grandchildren, and then I imagined how Daddy was probably getting to hug Davis again. Soon the children arrived, and all I could think about was how much I loved Daddy and what a wonderful life we shared. God had been so faithful to us.

Brother Pettis Brewer was still serving as pastor of the Morgantown Church when Daddy passed away on May 19, 1989. He preached Daddy's funeral at the Morgantown Church, along with other Church of God ministers A. D. Rhodes, Robert Gambil, and our son-in-law Don Clark. Our grandchildren, Randy and Melanie, and daughter-in-law Brenda, played the musical instruments and sang for the service. A trio from the local church (Cindy Smith, Blanche Stringfield, and Diane Morgan) also sang one of Daddy's favorite songs. Daddy was then buried in the Morgantown Cemetery about a quarter-mile from our house. I believe there were seventeen preachers who attended Daddy's funeral. At the time of Daddy's death, he had held credentials in the Church of God longer than anyone else living at that time except for Brother Otis McCoy. Daddy was three months shy of his 88th birthday.

It was very difficult for me after Daddy died. Naturally I grieved for him, but I remembered what he had told me about mourning so much following Davis's death. I guess I might have mourned a little more than I did if I had known I would live as many more years as I have. But, my family and church stood by me and were a great support.

The most difficult thing that I faced was overcoming my fear of living alone. I had never spent a night alone in my life, except for one time while we were pastoring in Dunn. Even then I did not intend on staying by myself, but the two girls who were supposed to stay with me went to a meeting and I drifted off to sleep before they arrived at the parsonage. The next day I woke up to discover that the girls had found me sleeping and decided to go on to their house for the night. After Daddy died my children were with me at first. Since Maxine and June both lived away with their families, they spent some time with me. However, I dreaded the day that I was left at home alone. The boys (that is what I call my sons) were always in and out of the house, but they had families of their own to be with at night. I did all I could to keep from going to sleep that first night by myself. Even after I went to bed I prayed and prayed. I asked the Lord to be with me and help me, and He did.

Sometime after I had started staying by myself at night, I experienced two visions. Two well-dressed men came into my house through the back door and stood in my kitchen staring at me. At first I thought they were there to harm me, so I began talking to them and bragging on them, telling them how nicely they were dressed. They would look at one another and smile, but they never said anything to me. They just smiled. I then knew that they were not there to harm me, but soon they left. Later on two men came into my living room through the front door. This time we talked, but I cannot remember what was said. The men then walked out the front door and one turned around and asked me, "Can you tell me where Hollis Allred lives?" But before I could answer they had gone. I knew very well who Hollis Allred was and where he lived. He was a Church of God member living at Natchez, Mississippi. I cannot explain those visions, and some might simply dismiss them. Yet, it was after experiencing those two visions that I felt assurance of God's protection and was not afraid to stay alone at night. I have always thought that those two men were guardian angels that God allowed me to see in order to know that He was taking care of me. It has been over 15 years since Daddy's death, and I still live alone.

11

Travel on a Little Farther

After Daddy passed away, I wondered what I would do with myself. I was almost 88 years old. "What in the world is left for an old widow woman at my age?" I thought occasionally. Yet, I soon discovered that Daddy had ended his journey, but there was still work left for me to do. During that time we sang the song at church that said, "Ready to go, ready to stay." That was a good description of my feelings. I was ready to go and be with the Lord, and I was also willing to stay if that is what God willed. So, I decided that I would travel on a little farther in my journey until the Lord calls me home.

I continued to be active in my Sunday school class, tried to do all I could in encouraging people (especially the youth) in their service to the Lord, and I still enjoyed praying with people. Sometimes I went to church early so I could pray in a Sunday school room before service. Too, I liked to play the organ and would often do so as the people gathered for worship.

I attended the women's prayer meeting on Monday mornings and also accompanied them to an area nursing home in Columbia on Tuesday afternoons. Those of us who frequently went to the nursing home visitation were Emmie Beal, Hazel Bracey, Helen Butler, Lorena Gartman, Geneva Morgan, Lanell Morgan, Opal Morgan, Delean Pearson, Ethel Rials, JoAnn Robertson, Bethel Scarborough, Blanche Stringfield, and my daughter-in-law Ann

Williams. Sometimes we would pick up little Louis Morgan after school and he would accompany us older women to the nursing home too. There we spent time visiting each resident before reassembling in the dining hall. As the residents gathered for supper, we had devotions and sang songs. Usually Delean Pearson played the piano for us, but sometimes I was able to play as well. Often I testified, prayed, and played Christian hymns on my French Harp (harmonica). I laugh and tell people that I enjoyed going to the nursing home and visiting those old folks! But it was a good outlet of ministry for me. I looked forward to it each week.

I even took up a new occupation after Daddy passed away. Although it is unofficial, I am probably the oldest fireman (or is it fire woman?) in Morgantown! One day I noticed smoke coming from the back of my house. I quickly discovered that my water heater had caught fire and was spreading flames across the back of my house. I yelled out for my neighbors, but no one was around to hear me. I feared that if I went back inside to call the fire department I might not make it out again. So I decided there was just one thing to do: I had to put out that fire myself. I hooked up the water hose and began to spray my house down. Within a minute or two I had put out the fire. Soon my labor had caught the attention of others, but the fire was gone by then. So, life can still be interesting at age 100, especially if you are a fire woman.

The year after Daddy passed away, the Morgantown congregation honored me on my 89th birthday. They honored me on Sunday, September 16, 1990, and called it "Mamie Williams Day" in Morgantown. My family had charge of the service, and the choir consisted of all my descendents that were able to attend. My daughter-in-law Brenda played the piano and my daughter June played the organ. All of my living children spoke. (We missed Daddy and Davis not being with us anymore, but we also spoke of them on that day.) My children told several humorous stories that had happened to Daddy and me through the years, as well as other personal reflections. Our pastor at the time was Reverend James Gholson and his wife Brenda. On behalf of the church, they, along with our clerk Martin Bean, presented me with a nice plaque and love gift. The local newspaper also ran a large article about the occasion, particularly focusing on mine and Daddy's life and ministry together. It was really a special day for me, and I was very happy to share it with my family and church family.

Life was going as usual. I was keeping my normal routine, and enjoying visits from my family and church friends. I was as active as I could be. Then I suffered a set back in my health. I had a case of the shingles on the left side of my head, neck, and shoulder. I guess I came nearer to death then than at any other time in my life. I did not have my right mind for quite some time because of the severe pain and also the medication that I was taking. I spent five weeks in the hospital, and I hardly knew that I was in the world for most of that time. My family prayed for me and had their churches to pray for me as well. My pastor called the Morgantown Church to intercede on my behalf, even having a special prayer day at the church for me where they anointed a handkerchief with oil and prayed over it. Then they gave the handkerchief to my family. I all but went to the grave, and would have if prayer had not brought me through. The Lord heard those prayers and He delivered me. But it was not an easy recovery.

After I was able to come home from the hospital, my children had to do everything for me. I had to learn how to walk all over again. My son-in-law, R. C. Edwards, would hold me up and tell me where to put my feet. Slowly, and very slowly, I learned how to walk again. That is quite an accomplishment for a 90-something year-old widow woman! But I could have never accomplished any of it had my children not taken the time and patience to help me. I also appreciated the many visits from my pastor at the time, Reverend Raymond Aven. I know it must have been a great sacrifice to them, but I am glad that I have been able to travel on a little farther.

It took quite some time for me to get use to the pain in my head and neck. The shingles damaged my nerves, and I still suffer to some degree every day. Yet, it is not as bad as it was at the beginning. The Lord helps me each day. Each night as I go to bed, I talk to the Lord. I begin by saying the prayer I learned as a child and also taught to my children: "Now I lay me down to sleep, I pray Thee Lord my soul do keep. If I die before I wake, I pray Thee Lord my soul do take." Then I just spend time talking to the Lord and thanking Him for His blessings. His goodness to us all can never be comprehended. I praise Him daily for His wonderful blessings, and I plan to keep doing so as I travel yet a little father while on my journey home.

12

Seeing the End of the Road

After completing one full century of living, I realize that I have been afforded a wonderful blessing. Many people are never able to reach such a milestone in their life, especially to be as independent as I am. That health ordeal, in addition to failing eyesight, has certainly slowed my pace. I am not able to do all that I could before, but I believe I am still fairly active for a 100-year-old woman. I am happy to be able to still live by myself and care for myself. I am now the oldest resident of Morgantown, and the oldest member of the Morgantown Church of God. I suppose that I am also one of the oldest members of the Pentecostal movement in Mississippi. I still enjoy attending church and have a desire to do all that I can for the work of the Lord. I also have time to pray for people, and spend much time each day doing just that. I pray for my family, the church, people in the community that I know are not living for the Lord, and for God's Spirit to flow throughout the world and bring revival to all nations.

I have a typical daily routine of waking at about 6:30 each morning. I look forward to cooking breakfast for my sons who live nearby. I did this every morning as long as my health permitted, but it is less frequent now. However, my boys still have breakfast with me. (After 100 years I guess it is time to finally let someone else do the cooking.) Before my health failed this past year I always served breakfast by about 7:30, when my son Flavous drops in for a visit. My favorite things to cook have always been eggs and biscuits. We enjoy breakfast together and then one of us will wash the dishes. By that time my son Charles usually stops by. We all sit and visit, often reminiscing about the past as well as discussing current issues such as politics, the news, what is happening in our community, and church activities. My son Howard usually drops in at some point during the day. It is convenient for them to visit so often because Flavous and Charles both live in Morgantown and Howard lives in nearby Columbia.

I also have frequent visits from Lavern, my daughter-in-law and Davis's widow. She has been a great friend to me, and I look forward to her visits. I also look forward to visits from my son Royce and his wife Elizabeth, as well as from my other son Darius and his wife Brenda. My daughters come to visit me quite often as well, and they usually stay several days at the time. Maxine and R.C. come from Texas, and June and Don come from Florida, where they pastor. I appreciate my family and my in-laws. I am also thankful that my family works for the Lord and supports the church. Right now I am enjoying the fifth generation of the Williams family and have over 125 descendants.

So, I am not alone or forgotten. Opal Morgan, a neighbor, visits me too. She often tells me that I have more company than anyone else in Morgantown, and I just laugh and tell her that it is all my family! I enjoy those visits from Opal, as well as from Doris Pearson, another neighbor. We always spend time in prayer before they leave, and Doris has read the weekly Sunday school lesson to me for many years since my eyesight has failed. I also enjoyed visits from Gladys Stringfield until her death in 2000. Gladys was one of the daughters of Sister Clara Priest and the mother of Flavous's wife, Ann. Gladys was more like a sister to me than anyone else in Morgantown. As long as she could drive her car, she came to see me. Even after that she always called me. I miss her so much.

Since I cannot see to read, most of my entertainment comes from watching television. Usually, I only watch Christian television and the news. I cannot see everything clearly, but I enjoy listening. "The 700 Club" with Pat Robertson is one of my favorite shows because it offers the news from a Christian perspective. I also enjoy listening to John Hagee, and I often finish my day by listening to the wonderful teaching of Charles Stanley, a Baptist pastor in Atlanta, Georgia. My favorite television preacher is Joel Osteen. He is a young preacher from Houston, Texas. He is so calm, happy, and reassuring. The television is company for me, and it encourages me to be able to hear the message of Jesus at any time of the day.

Once I was sitting in a grocery store waiting on my son and a man came and sat next to me. He asked me if I was Pentecostal and I told him that I was. He suggested that I had been in the holiness way for a long time, and I agreed that I had. Then we talked on about the Lord and His goodness. When I told the man about something I had heard on Christian television, he seemed shocked that I watched television. "Sure I do," I explained. "You can learn a lot, and the Word of God is being spread all over the world as a result." And that is what is important, that the message of our precious Jesus is being taken too all creatures throughout the world.

Although I enjoy Christian television, I still love going to church. I attend Sunday school and morning worship every Sunday that I can. My son Charles is now one of my Sunday school teachers. Occasionally I am able to go for evening services, but it is difficult for me to be out after dark. Nonetheless, I still enjoy being in the house of the Lord. I sit on the third row from the front, where Daddy and I always sat. There are two rows packed with teenagers who sit right in front of me, so I still feel connected with the young people. Opal Morgan usually sits with me, and my pink shawl is always tossed over the pew where I sit. (Older people get cold sometimes, you know.)

We have such wonderful services at Morgantown Church. We still enjoy the liberty to worship the Lord and are seeing many souls won to the Lord. Our pastor is Brother Salone Green, and his wife Jane is also a preacher. Sometimes it feels like old times when the Holy Spirit sweeps through. Much has changed in the church, but the Lord is still revealing Himself in power and mercy. I am blessed to have been able to see the Pentecostal blessing fill the earth as it has in these last days. The Holy Spirit is doing wonderful things throughout the world, and I am humbled to think that I have had a part in this movement.

Every day I walk throughout the rooms of my little house and bless the Lord. I sing and pray and rejoice in His goodness. I spend lots of time praying in the Holy Spirit and speaking in tongues.

What I received from the Lord as a young girl in Vardaman, Mississippi, is just as real to me today as it was on the first day that I received the blessing.

Since I became a Christian over 85 years ago, I have never felt like going back on the Lord. He has been too good to me and helped me in so many ways. I began working for the Lord in the ministry before I married. Even though it was not so much, I did what I could for the Lord. He has certainly blessed my family—eight loving children who are all saved by the grace of God and working in their churches.

I am so thankful that God's grace and power are with us. Back in the days when Pentecost was new, especially in Mississippi, we suffered many hardships for the Lord because people did not fully understand. Yet, we were willing to do it for the Lord. I am so thankful for my husband, who was faithful in ministering, establishing churches and pastoring in several states. I am thankful that God blessed us with a good life together and we were able to win souls to the Lord. I am thankful that God, by His grace and His Spirit, allowed us to witness to many people in six states and thousands of people in all of those churches.

We had many rules and regulations back in the early days that people could not understand, but we did the best we could with the understanding that we had of the Word of God. For instance, once we thought that it was a sin for a woman to cut her hair. While I do not believe that now, I still have long hair. It has never been cut in my life. I considered cutting it a few years ago, but then I decided that I had lived with it for over ninety years and may as well keep it as it is. Since then I have told my children that being a young girl (and I lived a single life for 22 years) those rules and the regulations were a hedge around me that kept me safe. I knew that if I stepped outside those rules I would not be doing right. I am thankful that today I still have that desire in my heart to be faithful. However, I am glad to know that we have learned that some things are not as important as we once thought.

Regardless of our early misconceptions, I am thankful for how God has used the Church of God and the souls that are being one to the Lord through its ministries. You know, I realize that we are just a small part of the Body of Christ, but we saw the vision from the very beginning and it is wonderful today to see what God is doing throughout the world and how people are accepting Him. It thrills my soul to know that God is still blessing people by His Spirit and power. It might not be exactly the same as it was back then, but the Lord is moving in just as powerful of a way today. There was a price that some had to pay to bring this full gospel to the world, but just look at what God is doing through His Body!

Now it seems that if you are not of Pentecost, or at least have a Pentecostal experience (saved, sanctified, and baptized with the Holy Ghost), you are just about out of style. But it certainly was not so back in the early days of our ministry. Oh, but I am thankful that I have lived to see the day that ministers and members do not have to suffer as the older ones did!

It is wonderful to know that souls were being won to the Lord and brought into the Kingdom all during those years of our ministry. We had many friends, and I still get mail from friends we made 40 and 50 years ago. Occasionally they will even include a little extra love gift—something that most of them did not have when we were pastoring them. It is wonderful to know that you can have good friends who, even after forty or fifty years, still think about you.

I wish that I could do more for the Lord now, and I would if I had my eyesight and better health. But my affliction has hindered me in my recent service to the Lord. Nonetheless, I still love Jesus and want to be true and faithful to Him until He calls me home. I often think about all of the many friends that I have made throughout the country during the years and how I would love to be able to sit and visit with them again. But, I know that we will be able to enjoy that friendship when we all get to Heaven. I like to sing that song many times because I am reminded of friends and Christian people that we have known along life's way and how we will be able to fellowship together again in Heaven.

Until I got married I had a Sunday school class of about thirty young people, and today so many of them have gone on to be with the Lord and I am still left here. Sometimes I do not understand why, but I want to be faithful and have the love of God in my heart so that people will know that there is a real joy in living for the Lord and in serving Him—even at age 100. I feel like I am ready to go because I realize that the end of time as we know it is near. I wish that all people would realize that the time is so near for the Lord to come back and rule and reign on this world again. That fills my heart with such joy and expectation!

If I could say anything to the Body of Christ today, I would encourage Christians to dedicate themselves to a regular prayer life and study of the Scriptures. Prayer and consecrated living are the things that brought the Church to where it is today. And it is prayer and dedication to God and to His Word that will move the Church forward. We have to be faithful to Jesus and have a burden for souls. It hurts me when I see people who claim to be Christians today who seemingly have no burden for lost souls. That should be our aim and desire—winning the lost to the Lord. We must have a burden to reach the lost because the coming of the Lord is so near at hand. It grieves me to know that there are people yet who do not know about our blessed Jesus—about how they can be saved and escape the things that are coming on the world today. We see so many things happening today that years ago we did not understand. But the Scriptures are being fulfilled right before our very eyes. I am happy to be living in this day to see some of the Scriptures being fulfilled that we did not understand in the beginning. How exciting! Yet, I grieve over the lost souls today who do not seem to be interested or do not seem to care whether they know anything about God or not. I may not be able to do much for the Lord any more, but I am praying for a revival that will stir this world for Jesus like it has never been stirred before.

Once I was asked about my secret to longevity. I believe it is good, clean living and a heart wholly consecrated to the Lord. I was also asked what advice I would give others, to which I offered, "Accept the Lord as your Savior, manifest his love to others and be faithful until death." Those are the things that I have tried to do in my lifetime, and I hope to one day hear the Lord tell me that I have done them well. I encourage others to find their place in the Kingdom of God and allow the Holy Spirit to form them into a witness for the Lord. Not all will be teachers, not all will be preachers and not all will be singers, but everyone has a work to do for the Lord. I found my place of ministry in 1920 and have tried to let the Lord accomplish that work through me. He has done more through me than I could have ever done on my own. I pray that everyone who reads these pages will be inspired to let the Lord do the same through them.

Often in life we find ourselves in circumstances where it is painful to look back on that from whence we have come. Yet, as one grows older the ability to look back and remember the good times offers comfort. I have reached that place in my life where I am happy to look back and remember the many ways that the Lord has blessed and provided. It only strengthens my faith in Him Who does all things well in His own time. But I am not one who only wants to look back, I am also eager to look forward. I can see the end of my journey ahead, and there is no fear or apprehension. I have excitement and anticipation, for I know that good things are in store for me. The Lord Who guides my steps is with me still, even after my one hundred years of walking with Him. To think about how wonderful the past has been and the present is now, I can only imagine the glory that the future holds. So I rejoice in the Lord today, thanking Him for my family, friends, and ministry.

At my 100th birthday celebration one of my great-great grandchildren reasoned out my purpose for still being alive. Little five-year-old Brenda asked her mother, "Why has Mamaw Williams lived so long?" Then, in her usual way, she answered her own question, "Oh, I know! It is because God knows that she is still telling people about Jesus!" I am not sure if that is the real reason that I am still alive after more than one hundred years, but that is certainly my goal for as long as I live. I plan to keep telling others about the goodness of the Lord and His saving grace, whether it is someone in the doctor's office, grocery store, one of the nurses who visits me weekly, or anyone else I might happen to meet along my journey. I do not plan to give up ministering until the Lord says it is enough and beckons me home. Rather, as I continue on my journey home I plan to go witnessing and rejoicing all the way.

Appendix

Letters and Sermons From the 'Church of God Evangel'

Request for Prayer

Dear *Evangel* Readers Everywhere:

I am not a member of the Church of God, neither does the Holy Ghost abide.

I joined the Baptist church a number of years ago and have since been trying to live a life that would please God. But, friends, I haven't done enough yet. Since I began reading the *Evangel* I have seen more of the light of God. I want the saints one and all to pray earnestly for me that the Holy Ghost may abide and speak in other tongues. As the Spirit gives the utterance.

My heart's desire is to be a true and shining light for my Savior and lead lost souls to Him. I realize that the coming of Christ will not be long and Oh! How my heart aches for those that are lost. I want the power of God so that I can tell the lost world more about our precious Savior.

Oh! Friends, pray for me that I may have this blessed experience that leads our souls to know more about Christ.

I am seeking full salvation and hope to soon let the *Evangel* readers know that I have it.

Love to all,
Mamie Parker

Church of God Evangel — June 5, 1920

Mamie Parker, Vardaman, Miss., requests the saints to pray that church will be established there and that she may stand true and hold out the light to the young boys and girls in her community.

Church of God Evangel — September 18, 1920

Brother G. C. Dunn and E. M. Washam have just closed a meeting at Taylor school house, near Vardaman, Miss. The Lord blessed them in giving out the Word. Several were saved and sanctified and five received the Holy Ghost with the Bible evidence of speaking in tongues, sixteen were added to the Church of God, others were looking and seeking this way. Eternity will only reveal the good done by these two Spirit filled preachers.

Your humble sister in Christ,
Mamie Parker,
Vardaman, Miss.

Church of God Evangel — March 5, 1921

REPORT

Brother E. M. Washam and Sister Mildred Biggers held a few days meeting here at Taylor, Miss., and in an adjoining community. The Lord wonderfully blessed them in giving out the Word. There was much shouting, dancing, and talking in tongues, a few were really convinced on holiness. There were 2 sanctified, 1 baptized with the Holy Ghost and 8 added to the Church of God.

Eternity alone can reveal the good that was done.

A sister who needs prayer,
Mamie Parker,
Vardaman, Miss.

Church of God Evangel — September 30, 1921, page 2

Doers of the Word and not Hearers Only

Dear *Evangel* Readers—
Greetings, Love and Peace be Multiplied Unto You All:

Beloved, I praise my Redeemer for showing me the light and because I have accepted it and am walking in it as it shines upon me.

I am so glad because I really have the victory. Hallelujah! It means something to have the victory each day in the week. But, praise God, I am glad of the experience that keeps me three hundred and sixty-five days in a year.

"Be doers of the word, and not hearers only, deceiving your own selves." James 1:22. Praise God, I want to be a doer and not a hearer only. I realize God's children need to measure up to "thus saith the Word of God" more and be real Bible Christians. It is my heart's desire to live humble and true so the world will know that there is some reality in the religion I profess. "Let us labor therefore to enter into that rest." Heb. 4:11. Beloved, I feel a work for me to do, and I am persuaded to believe we will have to strive to enter in. Brother and sister, are we striving as we should? Bless God! I want to live so in this life that when I press my dying pillow I may feel the very atmosphere of heaven hover around, and hear the sweet words of Jesus when He welcomes the redeemed in.

The Bible tells me of a land that flows with milk and honey that God has reserved for you and me and Jesus waits to make it free.

And there a river flows clear as crystal; on either side a tree of life with fruit and leaves to heal the strife. There is no night but one glad day.

There are other things I'd like to know, that's why I long to go. And soon I'll reach that country fair; by grace divine I'm going there!

Sometimes I feel like Paul, Phil. 1:23, "For I am in a straight betwixt two, having a desire to depart, and be with Christ, which is far better." Seems like heaven is all around me tonight and I am glad Jesus didn't die in vain for me.

I'm not only willing to believe on His name but to suffer for His sake.

I again ask God's children to lift me up to a throne of grace.

Your unworthy Sister,
Mamie Parker
Vardaman, Mississippi

Church of God Evangel — January 7, 1922

A Message For Your Heart

How many unhappy, sad and hungry hearts there are in the world! Sin crushes hearts and drags them down to death everywhere. But God speaks to you and He has a special message for you.

God loves you because He knows how sinful and wretched and unhappy you are deep down in your heart, however gay you may seem to be. Jesus Christ, the Son of God, loves you. When He was on earth He was known as a friend to sinners. He is acquainted with your life. When you were a child and your mother told you about Jesus, and when you grew up and first went into sin. He looked sorrowfully upon you and longed to win you from the snares and pitfalls of sin when you did not know that He was near you. His unseen presence is always with you—the presence of the Son of God, who wore a crown of thorns and died on the cross that your sins might be washed away in His precious blood. Just now, as you read these words, He is standing close beside you, whispering to your heart. Will you listen to His gentle voice?

Jesus wants to save you from hell, which is the penalty for sin. He wants to save you from sin in this life and lift you up to Himself. He died that your sins might be washed away and then, through a long eternity, that you might live with Him in bright mansions above. It is Jesus who offers you so much. Jesus! Jesus! Do you know how sweet that name may become to you? Do you know that He will enter your heart and dwell with you so that at any moment you may speak to Him and He will answer you? You may always look up into His face and see Him smile upon you.

Oh! it's Jesus that sinners need. Then there will be no more heart hunger; no desire for sin (for He makes us hate sin); no unsatisfied longings, for all desires and hopes are met in Him.

This same Jesus, who loves you, is soon coming back to earth again. When He was here before He was despised and rejected but He is coming again in the clouds and with great glory; coming in brightness and beauty to take His weary children home. When He went away, He said He would come again and receive us unto Himself. Do you want to be one of those who will welcome Him? When the skies shall rend and He shall descend in glory do you not want to say, "This is our God, we have waited for Him?"

Beloved, take this home to your heart.

Your sister under the blood,
Mamie Jane Parker,
Vardaman, Miss.

Church of God Evangel — November 18, 1922, page 4

A Progressive Sunday School

I would just like to tell a little about our Sunday school at Taylor church. It has a number one Sunday school with eighty-five enrolled. All love the Church and its cause. We remember the orphans every Sunday and have our penny march and pay our pennies.

Class No. 2, of which I am teacher, never fails to respond. In this class we have thirty boys and girls enrolled, ranging from fourteen to twenty years. This class is taught to help the orphans and

Foreign Missions. One of the boys recited the piece, China's Need. Then the class marched and paid their bit which amounted to $4.00. This class loves the Chinese and asks a blessing on those who are telling them the simple story of Jesus.

Yours for His cause,
Mamie Parker
Vardaman, Mississippi

Church of God Evangel — July 7, 1923, page 3

REPORT

The Church of God at Taylor reports victory. Children's Day was called for the third Sunday in June. It was a day of rejoicing for both young and old. The children spoke their pieces well. All seemed to honor "Him whom my soul loveth." A collection was taken for the orphans which amounted to $8.00. Many seemed to realize that the Church of God must do more for the orphans. Our pastor, J. E. Wigginton, preaches the Bible rightly divided and he believes in His church doing something for the orphans. God bless the orphans. We love them every one and our aim is to stand by them.

Mamie Parker
Vardaman, Mississippi

Church of God Evangel — July 7, 1923, page 2

Photographs

Presently, I am the oldest member of the Morgantown Church of God and the oldest resident of the Morgantown Community. Daddy and I first moved here when he was appointed State Overseer of Mississippi in 1931. We later retired here in 1961.

In addition to church work, I had a large family to love and care for. My children were always my first priority. Below is a photo taken in 1943. Front row, from left are:daughter Maxine, me, daughter June, Daddy, and son Darius. Back row, from left are:sons Charles, Davis, Flavous, Royce and Howard.

Daddy was an early student at the Church of God Bible Training School in Cleveland, Tennessee. His first term was in November 1918, which was actually the second term of the school. The teacher, Mrs. Nora Chambers, is seated on the front row, first from left. Daddy is standing in the back row, second from right. Standing next to Daddy is his good friend J. Oscar Hamilton. Daddy and Oscar were from the same town in Mississippi.

This is the Church of God General Assembly Auditorium and delegates in Cleveland, Tennessee. This photo was made before Daddy and I married, but he attended and I know where he is standing in this picture.

This is the Tomlinson House in Cleveland, Tennessee. It was located on Gaut Street across the road from the Church of God Publishing House, where Daddy first attended classes at the Bible Training School. This is the house Daddy and I stayed in when attending the General Assembly in 1923.

Above left is Bishop A. J. Tomlinson and his family. He was the first General Overseer of the Church of God and the the overseer when I first joined the church. Front row, from left are:Bishop Tomlinson, son Milton, and wife Mary Jane. Back row, from left are:daughter Iris, son Homer, and daughter Halcy. Bishop Tomlinson later served as General Overseer of the Church of God of Prophecy.

Above right is Bishop Flavius J. Lee, the second General Overseer of the Church of God. Daddy and I named our second son, Flavous, after him.

(L-R):M. S. Lemons and M. S. Haynes were early Church of God preachers. Before I married I assisted both of them in revivals and evangelistic meetings throughout Mississippi. Brother Haynes was the first State Overseer of Mississippi. Daddy and I named our oldest son, Davis Haynes, after him and another preacher, J. A. Davis.

Morgantown, Mississippi, Church of God
The above photo, taken in 1939, is the way the church looked when Daddy and I first visited the community for the state convention in 1923, as well as when we first moved to Morgantown in 1931 when Daddy was appointed State Overseer.

Below is the Morgantown church in 1945. This was the first brick Church of God sanctuary in Mississippi. Daddy and I are in the middle row, second from right.

While Daddy pastored the Morgantown Church of God we had a wonderful seven-week revival in 1947. Following that we needed more room for Sunday school classes. The extension on the right, which housed two classes, was built during Daddy's pastorate. The above photo was taken in 1949.

This is the present-day Morgantown church. I have many special memories of how God has blessed His children in this church. The church has experienced recent growth and is now in the process of building a new sanctuary.

On my 100th birthday, the Church of God honored me by placing my photograph on the cover of *AutumnLife* magazine for retired ministers and spouses. They also included an article about me, which was published in the *Church of God Evangel* as well. Brother Paul Henson and Geri, whom I consider dear friends, presented me with a framed copy of the magazine cover.

Dr. R. Lamar Vest, the General Overseer, also wrote me the kindest letter. My family and local church each had special celebrations for me. I felt so humbled and blessed to be honored in such a way. It is my desire in my remaining years to always lift up the standard of holiness and serve the Lord according to His Word.

Daddy and I celebrated our 50th Wedding Anniversary in 1973. If God was ever involved in joining two people together, I know He placed us together. We had such a happy life.

This is my 102nd birthday celebration held at the Morgantown church. In this photo I am with my children (standing, L-R) Royce, Maxine, Howard, June, Charles, and Darius. Seated next to me is my son Flavous. I currently have over 125 descendants, and I love them all. My prayer is that my family will always live for Jesus.

This photo was made during my 100th birthday celebration at the local church. I am thanking the congregation for their kindness, as well as sharing a little about God's failthfulness to me and exhorting them to go forward in the power of the Holy Spirit and win souls for the Lord. If we trust and obey the Lord, He will never fail us.

My pastor, Salone J. Green (left), and Brother Louis Morgan (right) after the church honored me at Morgantown Church of God on Sunday, September 16, 2001. Dr. R. Lamar Vest, our general overseer, sent me the kindest letter on behalf of the Church of God. Also, my beloved friends Paul and Geri Henson presented me with a framed photograph on behalf of the retired ministers' department. I am very thankful for all that the Church of God does for me.

Here I am with Louis Morgan, who has taken such interest in my life and helped me record so many of my experiences. I have probably already forgotten so much, and it would take too many pages to tell all that I do remember. Nonetheless, I hope you are blessed by these few pages. God is so good to us all!

About the Author

Louis F. Morgan, a native of Morgantown, Mississippi, has enjoyed researching history for over 20 years. As a child, Morgan often visited relatives and neighbors, including Grant and Mamie Williams, and listened to them reminisce about their life's experiences.

Filled with the Holy Spirit at age 9, Morgan has been involved in ministry for 20 years, primarily preaching and teaching—including two years as Minister of Youth at his home church (1992-94). In 1993, at age 18, he was chosen as "Family Training Hour Director of the Year" for the Church of God in Mississippi. A licensed minister with the Church of God since 1997, Morgan is a member of the Morgantown, Mississippi, Church of God. He currently attends North Cleveland Church of God in Cleveland, Tennessee, and conducts visitation and worship services at a local nursing home. He is also a volunteer deputy with the Bradley County Sheriff's Office, serving in the Senior Visitation division and visiting homebound senior citizens each week.

Morgan presently serves as an instructor and the Librarian of Instructional Services for Lee University and the Church of God Theological Seminary in Cleveland, Tennessee. He is a 1998 graduate of Lee University, a 2001 graduate of the Georgia Archives Institute, and a 2002 graduate of The University of Tennessee, Knoxville. He formerly served as Curatorial Assistant at the Museum Center at Five Points and as Archivist of the Dixon Pentecostal Research Center (Church of God archives), both located in Cleveland, Tennessee. He is a member of the Society of American Archivists, and also serves as the Tennessee Key Contact Representative for that organization. A member of the Tennessee Library Association, Morgan serves as co-chair of the Public Relations Committee. Morgan is a charter member of the Historical Society of Church of God Movements, and serves as Executive Secretary and Treasurer. He is also a lifetime member of the Marion County, Mississippi, Historical Society.

A prolific writer, Morgan has several manuscripts and articles to his credit and is frequently published in the *Church of God Evangel* and *Church of God History and Heritage.* His previous book, *Memories of Moma*, was published by White Wing Press in 2000. Morgan also researches local church histories and makes presentations for church anniversaries and other special events.